OTHER TITLES OF INTEREST

BASIC & LOGO
in Parallel

by
S. J. Wainwright
B.Sc., Ph.D., M.I.Biol., C.Biol.

BERNARD BABANI (publishing) LTD
THE GRAMPIANS
SHEPHERDS BUSH ROAD
LONDON W6 7NF
ENGLAND

PLEASE NOTE

Although every care has been taken with the production of this book to ensure that any projects, designs, modifications and/or programs etc. contained herein, operate in a correct and safe manner and also that any components specified are normally available in Great Britain, the Publishers do not accept responsibility in any way for the failure, including fault in design, of any project, design, modification or program to work correctly or to cause damage to any other equipment that it may be connected to or used in conjunction with, or in respect of any other damage or injury that may be so caused, nor do the Publishers accept responsibility in any way for the failure to obtain specified components.

Notice is also given that if equipment that is still under warranty is modified in any way or used or connected with home-built equipment then that warranty may be void.

© 1988 BERNARD BABANI (publishing) LTD

First Published — January 1988

British Library Cataloguing in Publication Data
Wainwright, S. J.
    BASIC and LOGO in parallel.
    1. BASIC (Computer program language).
    2. LOGO (Computer program language).
    I. Title
       005.13   QA76.73.B3

    ISBN 0 85934 171 2

Printed and bound in Great Britain by Cox & Wyman Ltd, Reading

DEDICATION

*I dedicate this book to
Lin and Lindsay*

CONTENTS

INTRODUCTION

BASIC and LOGO are computer languages that were both developed during the 1960's.

BASIC was developed at Dartmouth College by John Kemeny and Thomas Kurtz. The name 'BASIC' is an acronym for Beginners All Purpose Symbolic Instruction Code.

LOGO was designed in Cambridge, Massachusetts. LOGO was originally designed by Seymore A. Papert, Wallace Feurzig, and Daniel Bobrow. For a number of years Seymour Papert was codirector of the Artificial Intelligence Laboratory at M.I.T., and was the head of its LOGO project, which is concerned with the use of computers in the education of children. LOGO has been further developed at M.I.T. and at the Department of Artificial Intelligence of the University of Edinburgh.

Both BASIC and LOGO were conceived as languages which would make the programming of computers easier and therefore more accessible to potential users.

However, whilst in a sense they shared the same raison d'être, the motivations behind their respective developments were different.

The design of BASIC owes much to FORTRAN. FORTRAN is a language widely used in science and engineering, and is used for computation involving mathematical calculations. It is a compiled language which means that the FORTRAN translator program first translates the whole program into machine language, which is then executed as a machine code program and is hence very fast. However, compiled languages are not suitable for interactive program development due to the necessity of the intermediate step of compilation before the program can be executed. FORTRAN was designed to be used for batch processing. The program and data were stored on punched cards which were read by the machine via a special card reader input device. Moreover, input and output by FORTRAN programs was controlled by powerful but cumbersome FORMAT statements that proved very confusing to novices.

BASIC was developed as a language similar to FORTRAN in many ways but more friendly to use. BASIC was developed as an interpreted language which means that each line of the program is first translated into the machine language and is then executed. This means that the whole program does not have to be correct before it can be run. When the program is run, the interpreter will execute it line by line until either the end of the program is reached, or an error is encountered. This means that programs can be developed and tested in an interactive way at the terminal. BASIC has simplified free-format data input and output. This means that the BASIC programmer has less control over these processes than does the FORTRAN programmer, but the novice experiences no problems with them. (Modern versions of FORTRAN such as FORTRAN 77 have free-format data input and output as well as FORMAT statements, and most modern BASICs have some control over output via 'PRINT USING' statements.) BASIC is an allpurpose language but like FORTRAN, it is probably most suited to mathematical applications. However, BASIC does have simple yet powerful string-processing capabilities.

The design of LOGO owes much to the powerful list-processing language LISP that was also developed at M.I.T. However, LOGO was designed with ease of understanding and ease of operation in mind.

Modern LOGOs are finding applications outside what would have been originally envisaged for the language. However, it is important to understand the ideas behind the development of, and the use of LOGO.

The M.I.T. LOGO Project involves the M.I.T. Children's Learning Lab which is a computer-based learning environment in which research is carried out on the use of computers in the education of children. Seymore Papert eschews the use of computers to reinforce the traditional methods of education. For example, he argues that a student using a physics simulation to 'discover' the laws of physics, is interacting with the computer in a passive way. The computer program is very much in charge, and the student can 'discover' nothing but what the simulation is set up to enable him to discover. It is beyond the scope of this book to examine the debate on the use of computers in traditional syllabus teaching, but I personally have no doubt that there is a valuable role for computers in this area.

In the learning environment created by Papert, the pupil is in control of the learning situation rather than the program being in control. The pupil interacts with computer-controlled devices, experiments with them, and learns both from his/her successes *and* his/her failures (or surprises). One such device is the Turtle. Facilities for controlling the movements of the Turtle are fundamental to the LOGO programming language. The Turtle was so named in honour of a cybernetic animal made by the neurophysiologist Grey Walter. Early Turtles were electric mobile devices capable of turning and moving in any direction, and of either placing a pen on the surface over which they were moving or lifting the pen off the surface. They were connected by wires to the computer. The movements of the Turtle can be controlled by simple commands such as:

fd 100   or   FORWARD 100

which causes the Turtle to move 100 distance units in the direction it is facing. The Turtle can be made to change direction by using a command such as:

rt 45   or   RIGHT 45

which causes the Turtle to turn to its right through 45 degrees. If a command such as:

pd   or   PENDOWN

is given, then the Turtle will place its pen on the surface over which it is moving, and will thus draw a line.

In the early days of LOGO, computer graphics were very expensive to implement and so it was cheaper to make the Turtle a physical device as just described. Moreover, LOGO requires a lot of computer memory and so until the 1980's LOGO systems were expensive. Modern microcomputers have sufficient memory to be able to support useful implementations of LOGO. Moreover, the high resolution graphics capabilities of these machines means that the Turtle need no longer be a physical object. The Turtle exists on the screen and can be made to move around the screen in the same way that its physical predecessors moved around the floor. Screen Turtles have a variety of forms which range through actual turtle-shaped icons, circles with direction pointers, to arrowheads. With the proliferation of microcomputers in schools and homes, manufacturers have found it economic to manufacture low cost physical Turtles that can be controlled by some implementations of personal computer LOGO. It is likely that physical Turtles will be of greatest value in the classroom probably with younger children who will with greater ease, anthropomorphise the movements of the Turtle when they are working out how to draw certain geometric shapes. It is the screen Turtle however, that gives a wider potential to Turtle Graphics in the educational, scientific and even business fields.

Many people mistakenly believe that Turtle Graphics is the whole of LOGO. It is true that some of the smaller implementations of LOGO are restricted almost entirely to Turtle Graphics. However, a full implementation of LOGO will have powerful list-processing and mathematical capabilities. However, the simple syntax found in Turtle Graphics is preserved throughout LOGO.

BASIC is a simple language in the sense that its fundamentals are quickly learned and its concepts are uncomplicated. It was designed in this way so that newcomers to computer programming would quickly make progress and be able to produce programs that work. Seymore Papert criticises the *form* of simplicity of BASIC by likening it to a hypothetical language created by a master linguist such that it contains only 100 words. Of course, these words are very carefully chosen so that every possible thought could be spoken or written about. It could be argued that such a language would simplify language acquisition because its vocabulary would be learned very rapidly. However, people speaking or writing in this language would have a constant struggle against the constraints of the language. The difficulties would arise not in understanding the language itself, but in figuring out how to *say* anything even slightly complicated in it. This language might be simple in that it has a small vocabulary with primitive structures and concepts. The difficulty in *using* the language would be in proportion to the complexity of the ideas that one wished to express in it. A user of such a language would soon be looking for more powerful words with which to express his/her ideas, and to facilitate communication in a less tortuous manner. The user of the language would wish to *invent* new words. In BASIC, it is not possible to invent new words.

LOGO is a very different type of language from BASIC and in fact, it has a similar philosophy of program development to the computer language FORTH. In FORTH and in

LOGO, programs are developed in a modular way by the definition of new words. In LOGO, these words are called 'procedures'. The new procedures become part of the LOGO vocabulary, and can themselves be used in the definition of newer procedures still, and so on. Once defined, the new procedures have the same status as other procedures in the LOGO vocabulary and will execute when their names are entered. LOGO programmers tend not to think in terms of writing programs in the way that BASIC programmers do, but rather, in terms of the definition of new procedures that will perform specific tasks. The nearest that we can get to this in BASIC is to collect a library of subroutines or procedures which can be incorporated into future applications programs. Many BASICs have a 'MERGE' command that facilitates the linking together of pre-written segments of code. Programming in this way could be seen as writing and saving new routines, and linking pre-written routines together in the appropriate order.

Despite the substantial differences between BASIC and LOGO, this text takes both languages together, and investigates how things are done in each of them. As with all computer languages, there are a number of dialects of both BASIC and LOGO. Digital Research Inc's Dr.LOGO (Dr. LOGO is a trademark of Digital Research Inc.) is the version of LOGO used throughout this text. It is an extensive and powerful version of LOGO with Turtle Graphics, string-processing, and floating point arithmetic. As such, it has considerable potential for applications both inside and outside the classroom. Dr.LOGO is implemented on a number of microcomputers such as I.B.M., Tatung Einstein, and Amstrad.

BBCBASIC(Z80) by R.T. Russell is the version of BASIC used throughout this text. It is a version of BBCBASIC that runs on Z80 based machines such as Torch and Tatung Einstein microcomputers. There are only minor differences between this implementation of BBCBASIC and the original Acorn 6502 version. This dialect of BASIC was selected because it is one of the modern BASICs that uses procedures to which parameters can be passed, and within which local variables can exist. It is therefore, a suitable version of BASIC with which to make comparisons with LOGO. In fact, Sinclair's QL BASIC even has Turtle Graphics commands as well as procedures. However, at the end of this book is presented a listing of a powerful Turtle Graphics interpreter written in BBCBASIC(Z80). As Turtle Graphics commands are not a part of BBCBASIC, it will be much simpler to adapt the interpreter to other dialects of BASIC than if QL BASIC had been used.

In the following text, each example of LOGO is preceded by the word 'LOGO'. This is just to act as a reminder, and should not be typed into the computer. Similarly, each example of BASIC is preceded by the word 'BASIC'.

LOGO AND BASIC
IN IMMEDIATE MODE

LOGO and BASIC can both be used in immediate mode. That is, both the LOGO machine and the BASIC machine will execute commands as they are typed in without the necessity for the instructions to be part of a larger program. Thus, both LOGO and BASIC machines can be used in a sense as calculators although the commands that can be executed in immediate mode are not restricted to those concerned with arithmetic calculations.

BASIC uses the familiar algebraic notation of ordinary arithmetic. Thus, if we wished to multiply the numbers 2 and 3 in BASIC in immediate mode, and display the result, we would simply type:

        BASIC
        > PRINT 2*3

and the computer would print out:

        6
        >

(N.B. in BBCBASIC, the '>' symbol is the prompt given to indicate that the computer is ready. In many other versions of BASIC, the computer actually prints out the word 'READY'.) This type of algebraic notation is called *infix* notation. This is because the arithmetic operator '*' is fixed in between the numbers it is to operate on.

LOGO uses infix notation and it also uses the less familiar *prefix* notation. If we wish to multiply the numbers 2 and 3 in LOGO we could type:

        LOGO
        ?2*3   or   2 * 3

and the computer will print out:

        6
        ?

(N.B. in Dr.LOGO, the '?' symbol is the prompt given to indicate that the computer is ready.) It should be noted that spaces are used as separators in LOGO, so it is best to get into the habit of putting in spaces between numbers and operators or procedure names etc. to avoid problems later, even though the spaces can be omitted in arithmetic expressions as shown above.

It should be noted that in LOGO, it is only necessary to enter the expression e.g. '2 * 3', and the computer will print out the answer. However, one can use a 'print' command as in BASIC e.g.:

```
LOGO
?pr 2 * 3
```

and the computer will print out:

```
6
?
```

Note that the abbreviated form of 'print' i.e. 'pr' was used above. This is because in some implementations of Dr.LOGO, only the abbreviated form is recognised. The abbreviated form of procedure names will be used throughout this book, but the full name will be given the first time the procedure name is encountered.

When prefix notation is used in LOGO, then the numbers 2 and 3 could be multiplied together as follows:

```
LOGO
? * 2 3
```

and the computer will print out:

```
6
?
```

Alternatively, the 'print' command could be used as follows:

```
LOGO
? pr * 2 3
```

To illustrate the way that prefix notation arithmetic works we shall consider the following prefix notation arithmetic expressions:

```
LOGO
+ * 5 3 2
```

The computer will print out:

```
17
```

The interpreter starts with the last arithmetic operator i.e. '*', and performs that operation on the first two numbers i.e. 5 and 3. The result is 15. Thus at this stage, the expression is reduced to:

```
+ 15 2
```

The interpreter then performs the '+' operation on the numbers 15 and 2, returning the result 17. Similarly:

```
LOGO
* + 5 3 2
```

produces the result 16.

Infix and prefix arithmetic can be mixed in a single expression e.g.:

```
LOGO
2 * * + 5 3 2
```

returns the result 32. This is produced because the infix part of the expression '2 *' acts on the prefix part of the expression '* + 5 3 2', which we have just seen returns 16 as its result. Therefore, the above expression reduces to the infix expression:

```
2 * 16
```

which of course, returns a result of 32.

Numbers in BBCBASIC and Dr.LOGO

BBCBASIC and Dr.LOGO both use floating point arithmetic. However, in Dr.LOGO, *all* numbers are of type real. Numeric functions in Dr.LOGO evaluate to 16 significant figures, e.g.:

22 / 7   returns a value of   3.14285714285714;

1e6 * 22 / 7   returns   3142857.14285714;

and,

1e15 * 22 / 7 returns   3.14285714285714e+15.

In BBCBASIC, numbers can be either of type real or type integer. Arithmetic operations perform quicker on integers than on reals. Numeric functions evaluate to 9 significant figures e.g.:

PRINT 22/7   returns a value of 3.14285714;

PRINT 1E6*22/7   returns   3142857.14; and,

PRINT 1E15*22/7 returns   3.14285714E15.

In BBCBASIC, real numbers have a range of +−5.9E−39 to +−3.4E38. Integers on the other hand, have a range of +2147483647 to −2147483648.

Arithmetic in BBCBASIC
In BBCBASIC, there are seven arithmetic operators:

+	addition,
−	subtraction,
*	multiplication,
/	division,
∧	exponentiation.
MOD	returns the signed remainder of an integer division. Thus: PRINT 25 MOD 4 returns a value of 1.
DIV	returns the integer quotient of a division. Thus: PRINT 25 DIV 4 returns a value of 6.

The order of priority of arithmetic operations follows a fixed hierarchy which can be overridden by the use of parentheses.

Exponentiation has the highest priority and is done first.

Multiplication, division, DIV and MOD have the same priority, which is below exponentiation, but above addition and subtraction.

Within a given level of priority, the expression is evaluated from left to right. Thus:

PRINT 25 DIV 4/2

returns a value of 3, which shows that the DIV was done first. Note that the priority can be overridden by the use of parentheses. For example:

PRINT 25 DIV (4/2)

returns a value of 12, which shows that the / was done first.

To demonstrate that the evaluation is from left to right within the expression, and that DIV does not have a higher priority than / :

PRINT 80/8 DIV 3

returns a value of 3, which shows that the DIV was done last.

Arithmetic in Dr.LOGO
In Dr.LOGO, there are just the four arithmetic operators: + , − , * , and / . They have the same order of priority as in BBCBASIC, and as before, the priority can be overridden by the use of parentheses.

It might seem therefore, that Dr.LOGO is deficient in arithmetic operators when compared with BBCBASIC. In one sense this is true because only the four basic arithmetic operators are provided in the language. However, in another sense it is not true because as LOGO is an extensible language, other arithmetic operators such as DIV, MOD, and others can be added to the LOGO vocabulary should the user require them for his/her applications. In fact, we shall add several arithmetic operators to the LOGO vocabulary in a later section when we deal with extending the language as we develop programs. In another book in this series, 'BASIC and FORTH in Parallel' I wrote that there are as many versions of FORTH as there are users of FORTH. This is also true of LOGO.

11

Printing out Strings in BASIC

A string of characters can be printed on the screen by using a 'PRINT' statement as follows:

    PRINT"THIS IS A STRING"

Everything between the quotes is printed on the screen.

Positioning the Printout on the Screen

In BBCBASIC, the 'TAB' function can be used to determine the position of the printout on the screen. For example:

    PRINT TAB(20,12);"STRING"

will cause the string 'STRING' to be printed out in the middle of the screen. That is, starting in column 20, line 12. (The screen has 40 columns and 24 lines.)

When two parameters are passed to the 'TAB' function as above (i.e. the 20 and the 12), then the 'TAB' function behaves like the 'PRINT AT' statement in other BASICs.

If only one parameter is passed to the 'TAB' function, for example:

    PRINT TAB(15);"TEXT"

then the string 'TEXT' is printed out, starting in column 15 on whatever line the cursor is currently positioned.

A 'string' is a string of characters. In BASIC, a string is a structure of type character. BASIC 'knows' that the string is of type character, because the string is enclosed within quotes. Thus, in BASIC:

    PRINT 123

and:

    PRINT"123"

will both cause '123' to be printed on the screen. However, in the first case, the *number* 123 is printed out, and in the second case, the *string* '123' is printed out. Although the results look the same, the processes are different.

Printing out strings in LOGO

In LOGO, things work in a different way to BASIC. For example, if we try:

    pr "this is a string"

the computer will display:

    this
    I don't know how to is

This error message is given because spaces are used as separators by LOGO. LOGO interprets the line: pr "this is a string" as an instruction to print out the string 'this', which it does, and then an instruction to execute a procedure called 'is', so an error condition occurs, and the error message is generated.

In LOGO, strings are not enclosed in quotes. The 'pr' ('PRINT') procedure will print out everything that follows the quotes *until* a space is encountered. Thus, if we wish to use the 'pr' procedure in a way similar to a BASIC 'PRINT' statement, we can use a character such as an underline ' _ ' instead of a space, and produce quite readable text, e.g.:

    pr "this_is_a_string

will print out: 'this_is_a_string'. It should be noted that the trailing quotes are not used as in BASIC.

In LOGO, continuous strings of characters with no spaces among them, and preceded by double quotes, are called words. If we wish to print out a string of characters that includes spaces, then we must use a different type of data called a *List*. A List starts and ends with square brackets. The elements of a List are separated by spaces. The elements of a List can be numbers, words, or Lists. We can use 'pr' to print out a List, e.g.:

    pr [this is a list]

which would display:

    this is a list

We can see that 'pr' removes the outer square brackets of a list before it is displayed.

The 'pr' procedure can be used to print out numbers in a way rather like a 'PRINT' statement in BASIC, for example:

    pr 123

will cause '123' to be printed out, and:

    pr 123 456

will cause:

    123
    456

to be printed out.

Positioning the printout on the screen

    setcursor [2Ø 15] pr "String

will print the string 'String' in column 2Ø, line 15. The Procedure 'setcursor' takes a List containing the 'X' and 'Y' coordinates as its parameter. Similarly, a List could be printed out at the same screen position as follows:

    setcursor [2Ø 15] pr [A List]

There are two other Dr.LOGO procedures for printing to the screen, they are: 'type' and 'show' and they differ slightly from 'pr'. With the procedure 'pr' there is an inbuilt carriage return after the item is printed, thus:

    pr 23 pr 24

will display:

    23
    24

on the computer screen. Moreover, we have seen that 'pr' removes the outer square brackets from lists before they are

14

printed. The procedure 'type' behaves like 'pr' with the exception that there is no inbuilt carriage return after the item has been printed. Thus:

    type 23 type 24

will display:

    2324

If we wished to place a space between the '23' and the '24', then we would have to enter:

    type 23 "\ 24

which would display:

    23 24

In Dr.LOGO, the ' "\ ' forces LOGO to interpret a delimeter as a literal character. For example:

    type "dog "\ bite

will display:

    dog bite

because the ' "\ ' causes the space immediately before the word 'bite' to be regarded as a character rather than as a separator.

The procedure 'show' behaves exactly like 'pr' with the exception that the outer brackets of lists are not removed before they are printed. As with 'pr', there is an inbuilt carriage return after the item is printed. If we enter:

    show [this is a list]

the computer will display:

    [this is a list]

Assigning Values to Variables

In BASIC:
Values are assigned to variables by using the '=' symbol, which means 'becomes equal to', e.g.:

    SCORE=SCORE+1

which means: set the value of the variable 'SCORE' to the current value of 'SCORE' plus 1. In this example, the variable 'SCORE' is a real variable, that is, it can contain fractional parts. In BBCBASIC, numeric variables default to type real. It is possible however, to declare a numeric variable to be of type integer by placing the character '%' as a suffix to the variable name, e.g.:

    SCORE%=SCORE%+1

In this case, the variable 'SCORE%' is of type integer, and cannot contain numbers with fractional parts, e.g. if the following lines are entered:

    I%=5
    I%=I%/2
    PRINT I%

will result in '2' being printed out. In the first line, the value of '5' is assigned to the integer variable 'I%'. In the second line, the integer variable 'I%' is assigned the value of the current value of 'I%' divided by '2'. However, as 'I%' is an integer variable, the '0.5' is lost and so the value '2' is assigned to 'I%'.

Variables can be declared as being 'string variables', i.e. variables of type character by placing the character '$' as a suffix to the variable name, e.g.:

    PIG$="BACON"

which assigns the value 'BACON' to the variable 'PIG$'.

In LOGO:
Values are assigned to variables by using the procedure 'make',

e.g.:

    make "pig "bacon

which assigns the value 'bacon' to the variable 'pig'. It should
be noted that the spaces are important in LOGO as they are
used as separators. The quotes before 'pig' tell LOGO that
what follows is an object and not the name of a Procedure.
If we enter the line of LOGO as above and then enter:

    pr :pig

then the computer will print out:

    bacon

The colon before 'pig' means 'output the value of the variable
whose name follows'. Thus, the value of 'pig', i.e. 'bacon' is
output to the procedure 'pr', which prints it out. If the 'pr'
is omitted as follows:

    :pig

then the computer will print out:

    bacon

because the colon causes the output of the value of 'pig'.
If there is no procedure for the colon to output a value to,
then the value is output to the screen. We could however,
assign the value of 'pig' to another variable by the use of a
colon as follows:

    make "meat :pig

If we were then to enter:

    :meat

the computer would print out:

    bacon

17

There is another way of obtaining the value of a variable, and that is by the use of the procedure 'thing'. The procedure 'thing' behaves like a colon but has extra capabilities. If we enter:

    thing "meat

then the computer will print out:

    bacon

just as it did when the colon was used. The procedure 'thing' outputs the value of the variable whose name follows. However, the following would be possible with 'thing', but could not be done with colons:

    make "dog "hound
    make "canine "dog
    pr thing thing "canine

and the computer would print out:

    hound

If we tried to do the same thing with colons by entering:

    make "dog "hound
    make "canine "dog
    pr ::canine

then the computer would print out:

    :canine has no value

This is because the first colon treats what follows, i.e. ':canine' as a variable name, which of course, does not exist. However, it could be the case that a variable called ':canine' had been previously assigned. In which case, no error would arise, but confusion would! E.g., suppose the following were entered:

    make ":canine "terrier
    make "dog "hound
    make "canine "dog
    pr ::canine

the computer would print out:

    terrier

  LOGO is very 'friendly' about variable types. The type of
a LOGO variable is the type of the current value. Thus it is
quite possible to successively assign values of different types to
a given variable as follows: (which would be quite impossible
in BASIC):

    make "variable 42
    make "variable 1Ø.5
    make "variable "fish
    make "variable [animal vegetable mineral]

With each new value assignment of the variable 'variable',
the type of the variable changes.

Standard Library Functions in BASIC
Standard Library Functions are provided in both BASIC and
LOGO (although they are not usually called Library Functions
in LOGO).
  In BASIC, a Standard Library Function performs a pre-
scribed task on a specified *parameter* which is usually enclosed
in parentheses. The Standard Library Functions of BBC-
BASIC are given below in alphabetical order:

ABS e.g.,

    PRINT ABS(Y)

prints out the absolute value of the number contained in the
variable 'Y'.

ACS e.g.,

    X=ACS(Y)

assigns the arc cosine of 'Y' to the variable 'X' (Y must be
expressed in radians). The relationship between degrees and
radians is as follows:

    radians=degrees*PI/18Ø   where PI=3.14159

19

ADVAL e.g.,

    TEMP=ADVAL(1)

There are four analogue to digital converter channels. The
A-D converter channel is specified by the parameter passed to
the ADVAL function e.g. '1' in the example above. The
channels each have a resolution of 8 bits, but the value
returned is scaled to 16 bits. If a parameter of Ø is passed
to the 'ADVAL' function, then the value returned indicates
which, if any, of the 'fire' buttons on a games paddle has been
pressed. For example:

    FIRE=ADVAL(Ø)

will assign a value to the variable 'FIRE' depending on which
button on the games paddle has been pressed. Thus:

    If FIRE=Ø, then no button has been pressed.
    If FIRE=1, then the left button has been pressed.
    If FIRE=2, then the right button has been pressed.
    If FIRE=3, then both buttons have been pressed.

ASC e.g.,

    PRINT ASC("S")

will print out the ASCII code (American Standard Code for
Information Interchange) for the letter 'S'. Thus the computer will print out '83'. If we had entered:

    PRINT ASC("STRING")

the computer would still print out '83'. The Function 'ASC'
will return the ASCII code for the first letter of a string unless
another Function such as 'MID$' is used to specify a particular
character in the string. For example:

    PRINT ASC(MID$("STRING",3))

will print out '82', which is the ASCII code for 'R', the third
character in the string 'STRING'. (See the Function
'MID$' which follows later.)

ASN e.g.,

    X=ASN(Y)

assigns the value of the arc sine of 'Y' to the variable 'X'. ('Y' must be expressed in radians.)

ATN e.g.,

    PRINT ATN(Y)

will print out the arc tangent of 'Y'. ('Y' must be expressed in radians.)

BGET# e.g.,

    BYTE=BGET#n

will get a byte from the data file whose channel number is 'n', and assign it to the variable 'BYTE'.

CHR$ e.g.,

    PRINT CHR$(84)

will print out 'T' which is the character specified by the ASCII code '84'.

COS e.g.,

    X=COS(Y)

assigns the cosine of 'Y' to the variable 'X' . ('Y' must be expressed in radians.)

COUNT e.g.,

    UNTIL COUNT=1Ø

'COUNT' returns the number of characters sent to the screen or the printer since the last newline.

DEG e.g.,

    X=DEG(Y)

assigns the value of 'Y' radians, in degrees, to the variable 'X'.

EOF# e.g.,

    IF EOF#n THEN . . .

will proceed to the statements after 'THEN' if the end of the file whose channel number is 'n' has been reached.

ERL e.g.,

    MISTAKE=ERL

will assign the line number where the last error occurred to the variable 'MISTAKE'.

ERR e.g.,

    CODE=ERR

will assign the error code of the last error to occur to the variable 'CODE'.

EVAL e.g.,

    X=EVAL(E$)

will use the BASIC expression evaluation routines to evaluate 'E$' where 'E$' is an arithmetic expression. The result is then assigned to the variable 'X'.

EXP e.g.,

    X=EXP(Y)

assigns the value of 'e' raised to the power 'Y' to the variable 'X' (where 'e' is the base of natural logarithms, 2.7182818).

EXT# e.g.,

    LENGTH=EXT#n

assigns the total length of the file whose channel number is 'n' to the variable 'LENGTH'. The value returned will always be an exact multiple of 128.

FALSE e.g.,

    PRINT FALSE

will cause a zero to be printed out. 'FALSE' is a function that returns the value of zero and this is then interpreted in a logical manner. Any value that is not zero is interpreted as NOT FALSE.

GET e.g.,

    BUTTON=GET

will wait for a key to be pressed on the keyboard, and then assign the ASCII value of the key to the variable 'BUTTON'.

GET$ e.g.,

    BUTTON$=GET$

will wait for a key to be pressed on the keyboard, and then assign the character of the pressed key to the string variable 'BUTTON$'.

' In both 'GET' and 'GET$', the parameter that is passed to the function is specified by the key that is pressed.

INKEY e.g.,

    BUTTON=INKEY(n)

waits for up to n*10ms and essentially does a 'GET' function. If a key is pressed during the specified time interval, then the ASCII value of the key will be assigned to the variable 'BUTTON'. If a key is not pressed during the specified time interval, then −1 will be assigned to the variable 'BUTTON', and the program will continue. The parameter 'n' can range from 0 to 32767.

INKEY$ e.g.,

    BUTTON$=INKEY$(n)

waits for up to n10ms and essentially does a 'GET$' function. If a key is pressed during the specified time interval, then the character indicated by the key will be assigned to the string variable 'BUTTON$'. If a key is not pressed during the specified time interval, then a null string is assigned to the variable 'BUTTON$', and the program will continue.

INSTR e.g.,

X=INSTR("FREDDY", "RED")

will assign '2' to the variable 'X' because the substring 'RED' starts at position 2 within the string 'FREDDY'. If the specified substring is not found, then a Ø is returned, and will be assigned to the variable 'X'.

INT e.g.,

PRINT INT(5.5)

will print out '5' which is the integer *below* the real number that is the parameter of the 'INT' Function. Similarly:

PRINT INT(5)

will also print out '5'. However:

PRINT INT(−5.5)

will print out '−6' because this is the integer *below* the real number '−5.5'.

LEFT$ e.g.,

PRINT LEFT$("LANDING",4)

will print out 'LAND', i.e. the left 4 characters of the string 'LANDING'.

LEN e.g.,

PRINT LEN("LANDING")

will print out '7', which is the length of the string 'LANDING' which is the parameter of the 'LEN' Function.

LN e.g.,

L=LN(X)

will assign the natural logarithm of 'X' to the variable 'L'.

LOG e.g.,

    L=LOG(X)

will assign the logarithm to the base 1Ø of 'X' to the variable
'L'.

MID$ e.g.,

    PRINT MID$("LANDING",4,3)

will print out 'DIN' which comprises 3 characters from the
string 'LANDING', starting at the 4th character. If the third
parameter of the 'MID$' Function is omitted, for example:

    PRINT MID$("LANDING",4)

then the 4th character of the string 'LANDING', and everything following it will be printed out. Thus, 'DING' will be
printed out.

OPENIN e.g.,

    N=OPENIN("FILENAME")

will open a disc file for reading or updating, and will assign
the channel number of the file (which has been 'decided' by
the computer), to the variable 'N'.

OPENOUT e.g.,

    N=OPENOUT("FILENAME")

will open a disc file for writing to, and will assign the channel
number of the file to the variable 'N'.

PI e.g.,

    PRINT PI

will print out 3.14159265.

POINT e.g.,

    PIXEL=POINT(X,Y)

will assign a value of '1' to the variable 'PIXEL' if the pixel at screen coordinates 'X', 'Y' is 'lit'. A value of '0' will be assigned to the variable 'PIXEL' if the pixel at the specified coordinates is 'unlit', and a value of −1 will be assigned to the variable 'PIXEL' if the specified coordinates are off the screen.

RAD e.g.,

    PRINT RAD(Y)

will print out 'Y' degrees in radians.

RND e.g.,

    PRINT RND(1)

will print out a pseudo-uniform random real number in the range $0.0 - 0.99999999$. It should be noted that 'RND(n)' returns pseudo-random number in the range $0.0 - n$.

SGN e.g.,

    A=SGN(Y)

will assign '+1', '−1', or '0' to the variable 'A' depending on whether 'Y' is respectively, positive, negative, or zero.

SIN e.g.,

    PRINT SIN(Y)

will print out the sine of 'Y'. ('Y' must be expressed in radians.)

SQR e.g.,

    PRINT SQR(V)

will print out the square root of 'V'.

STR$ e.g.,

    PRINT STR$(200)

will print out '200' because 'STR$' returns the string form of the numeric parameter.

STRING$ e.g.,

    PRINT STRING$(3,"Hello ")

will print out 'Hello Hello Hello '. That is, the string 'Hello '
will be concatonated 3 times.

TAN e.g.,

    PRINT TAN(Y)

will print out the tangent of 'Y'. ('Y' must be expressed in
radians.)

TOP e.g.,

    PRINT TOP

will print out the address of the first memory location after
the user's program.

    PRINT TOP-PAGE

will print out the length of the BBCBASIC program in memory.

TRUE e.g.,

    PRINT TRUE

will print out '−1' (see 'FALSE'). 'TRUE' is a numeric
substitute for a true Boolean variable, and its value of −1 is
interpreted in a logical manner. In practice, any value that
is not zero is interpreted as TRUE.

USR e.g.,

    PRINT USR(&EB3A)

will print out an integer value because 'USR' is a Function
which provides the programmer with a means of calling a
segment of machine code that is designed to return a single
value.

27

VAL e.g.,

>   PRINT VAL("3")

will print out '3'. The Function 'VAL' converts a character string in the form of a number to numeric form. It should be noted that 'VAL' will not deal with strings that represent hexadecimal numbers, nor will it perform any arithmetic as indicated by the string.

VPOS e.g.,

>   X=VPOS

will assign a value to the variable 'X' which equals the vertical position of the cursor.

Standard Library Functions in LOGO

In LOGO, it is not usual to talk about 'Library Functions'. LOGO words are called 'Procedures'. The Procedures that are supplied in the LOGO system are called 'primitives'. However, many of the primitives in LOGO are directly analogous to Standard Library Functions in BASIC in that they return some kind of 'value' usually depending on a parameter that is passed to the Function. The primitives of Dr.LOGO (the Einstein implementation) that parallel BASIC Standard Library Functions are given as follows in alphabetical order.

In the version of Dr.LOGO used here, in many cases, only abbreviated forms of the procedure names are recognised. Moreover, the procedure names are in lower case. For this reason, the abbreviated form of the procedure name will be given first in lower case, and then in full in upper case.

In order to facilitate the explanation of certain primitives, it will be necessary to assign values to certain variables. Within this section, once a variable has been assigned a value, it will be assumed to have that value for the purpose of illustrating subsequent primitives, unless of course, its value is changed by having a new value assigned to it. We shall begin by assigning the value 'bacon' to the variable 'pig' as follows:

>   make "pig "bacon

We shall now discuss the LOGO primitives that parallel Library functions:

28

and   **AND** e.g.,

> and (:pig="bacon)   (10>5)

will cause the computer to print out:

> TRUE

because the logical expression '(:pig="bacon)' *and* the logical expression '(10>5)' are *both* true. However, if we enter:

> and (:pig="pork) (10>5)

then the computer will print out:

> FALSE

because the first logical expression is not true.

arctan   **ARC TANGENT** e.g.,

> arctan 42

will print out:

> 88.636072468397

which is the arctangent of 42 degrees. If we assign the value '21' to the variable 'angle' as follows:

> make "angle 21

we can then find its arctangent as follows:

> arctan :angle

which will cause the arctangent of 21 to be printed out as follows:

> 87.2736890060935

ascii   **ASCII** e.g.,

> ascii "p

will print out:

> 112

which is the ASCII code for 'p'. Actually, the procedure 'ascii' returns the ASCII code of the *first* character of the input word, e.g.:

> ascii "pig

will still print out:

> 112

However, if we enter:

> ascii :pig

then the computer will print out:

> 98

which is the ASCII code for 'b' which is the first character of the word 'bacon' which is the *value* of the variable 'pig'.

bf   **BUT FIRST** e.g.,

> bf "abcde

will print out:

> bcde

that is, all of the input object *but the first* element. If the input object is a List, (i.e. a set of elements separated by spaces and surrounded by square brackets) e.g.:

> bf [ab cd ef gh]

then the computer will print out:

> [cd ef gh]

bl   **BUT LAST** e.g.,

> bl "abcde

will print out:

> abcd

The procedure 'bl' will print out all of the input object *but the last* element.

buttonp   **BUTTON PADDLE** e.g.,

> buttonp Ø

will print out either 'TRUE' or 'FALSE' depending on whether the button on paddle Ø is being pressed, or is not being pressed respectively. The second paddle is identified by the number '1'.

char   **CHARACTER** e.g.,

        char 98

will print out:

        b

because the ASCII code for 'b' is '98'.

cos   **COSINE** e.g.,

        cos 42

will print out:

        0.743144810199738

which is the cosine of 42 degrees. Similarly:

        cos :angle

will print out:

        0.93358039855957

which is the cosine of 21 degrees which is the value of the variable 'angle'.

cursor   **CURSOR** e.g.,

        cursor

will cause the computer to print out a List such as:

        [0 21]

which are the current coordinates of the position of the cursor on the screen.

dir   **DIRECTORY** e.g.,

        dir

will print out a List of the names of the LOGO files on the specified or default disc e.g.:

        [ARRAYS FUNCS]

This would indicate that there are two LOGO files on the disc, and that they are called 'ARRAYS.LOG' and 'FUNCS.LOG' respectively.

31

emptyp   **EMPTY PREDICATE** e.g.,

        emptyp :pig

will cause the computer to print out:

        FALSE

because the variable 'pig' is not an empty word or List. However, if we enter:

        make "a [ ]

and then enter:

        emptyp :a

the computer will print out:

        TRUE

because 'a' is an empty List.

equalp   **EQUAL PREDICATE** e.g.,

        equalp :angle 21

will cause the computer to print out:

        TRUE

because the current value of the variable 'angle' is '21'. If we were to enter:

        equalp [dog] [cat]

then the computer would print out:

        FALSE

first   **FIRST** e.g.,

        first "cat

will cause the computer to print out:

        c

which is the first element of the object 'cat'. Similarly, if we enter:

        first [dog cat]

the computer will print out:

dog

which is the first element of the List '[dog cat]'.

fput   **FIRST PUT** e.g.,

        fput "rat [dog cat]

will output:

        [rat dog cat]

whilst:

        fput [rat] [dog cat]

will output:

        [[rat] dog cat]

glist   **GETLIST** e.g.,

        glist ".DEF

could output for example:

        [average]

if the user-defined procedure 'average' is the only procedure that has been defined. This is because 'average' would have '.DEF' in its property list.

gprop   **GET PROPERTY** e.g.,

        gprop "angle ".APV

would cause the computer to print out:

        21

because '21' is the .APV (Associated Property Value) of the global variable 'angle'.

int   **INTEGER** e.g.,

        int 2.5

will output:

        2

Similarly:

int 12/5

will output:

2

which is the integer part of the input value. If we enter:

int −3.6

then the function will output:

−3

Note that LOGO differs from BASIC in this function because 'INT(−3.6)' would return '−4' in BASIC.

item   **ITEM** e.g.,

item 3 :pig

will output:

c

because 'c' is the third element in the value of the variable 'pig' (the value of 'pig' is 'bacon'). Alternatively:

item 3 "pig

will output:

g

which is the third element of the object 'pig'.

keyp   **KEYBOARD PREDICATE** e.g.,

keyp

will output:

FALSE

because no character has been typed at the keyboard and is waiting to be read.

last   **LAST** e.g.,

last "pig

will output:

g

because 'g' is the last element of the object 'pig'. Similarly:

last [cat dog rat]

will output:

rat

lput   **LAST PUT** e.g.,

lput "fish [cat dog rat]

will output:

[cat dog rat fish]

It can be seen that 'lput' makes the input object become the last element of a List.

list   **LIST** e.g.,

list "cat "dog

will output:

[cat dog]

That is, 'list' creates a List from the input objects by putting square brackets around them. As it stands, 'list' will only do this with two input objects. For example:

list "cat "dog "rat

will output:

[cat dog]
rat

However, if the whole line is enclosed by parentheses are follows:

(list "cat "dog "rat)

then long Lists can be created, and in the case above:

[cat dog rat]

would be output to the screen.

listp   **LIST PREDICATE** e.g.,

>   listp "pig

will output:

>   FALSE

However, let us define a List called 'insects' as follows:

>   make "insects [flies beetles]

Then if we enter:

>   listp :insects

the computer will output:

>   TRUE

because the value of the object 'insects' is the List [flies beetles].

lc   **LOWER CASE** e.g.,

>   lc CAT3

will output:

>   cat3

because all upper case letters have been converted to lower case.

memberp   **MEMBER PREDICATE** e.g.,

>   memberp "i "pig

will output:

>   TRUE

because 'i' is an element of the object 'pig'. Similarly:

>   memberp "flies :insects

will output:

>   TRUE

because 'flies' is an element of the value of the object 'insects', which we have previously defined as the List [flies beetles]. However, if we enter:

memberp "spiders :insects

then the computer will output:

FALSE

namep   **NAME PREDICATE** e.g.,

namep "vax

will output:

FALSE

because we have not declared a variable name to be 'vax'. However, if we enter:

namep "angle

then this will output:

TRUE

because we do happen to have a variable name called 'angle'.

nodes   **NODES** e.g.,

nodes

could output for example:

2305

which would be the number of free nodes in the LOGO workspace. In Dr.LOGO, one node takes up five bytes.

not   **NOT** e.g.,

not (:angle=42)

will output:

TRUE

because the value of the variable 'angle' is not equal to '42'. In fact, the value of 'angle' is '21', therefore:

not (:angle=21)

will output:

FALSE

numberp   **NUMBER PREDICATE** e.g.,

>numberp "cat

will output:

>FALSE

because the object 'cat' is not a number. However:

>numberp :angle

will output:

>TRUE

because the value of the variable 'angle' is a number. Whereas:

>numberp :insects

will output:

>FALSE

because the value of the variable 'insects' is not a number.

or   **OR** e.g.,

>or (numberp :angle)(numberp :insects)

will output:

>TRUE

because either the first logical expression (in brackets) is true *or* the second logical expression is true, (in fact, the value of the variable 'angle' is a number as we have seen above), so the first logical expression is true.

>or (numberp :pig)(numberp :insects)

will output:

>FALSE

because neither of the logical expressions in brackets is true.

paddle   **PADDLE** e.g.,

>paddle Ø paddle 1 paddle 2 paddle 3

would output the X coordinate of paddle 1, the Y coordinate of paddle 1, the X coordinate of paddle 2, and the Y coordinate of paddle 2 respectively.

piece   **PIECE** e.g.,

>   piece 2 4 :pig

will output:

>   aco

which are the second to the fourth elements of the value of the variable 'pig', which is 'bacon'. Similarly:

>   piece 2 3 "pig

will output:

>   ig

which are the second to the third elements of the object 'pig'.

pons   **PRINT OUT NAMES** e.g.,

>   pons

`could output for example:

>   insects is [flies beetles]
>   pig is bacon
>   angle is 21

That is, the names of all of the variables and their values are output.

plist   **PROPERTY LIST** e.g.,

>   plist "insects

would output:

>   [.APV [flies beetles]]

because 'plist' prints out the property list of the named object.

quotient   **QUOTIENT** e.g.,

>   quotient 11 2

will output:

>   5

which is the integer quotient of 11/2.

random   **RANDOM** e.g.,

> random 30

could output for example:

> 19

which is a random positive integer less than 30.

remainder   **REMAINDER** e.g.,

> remainder 11 2

would output:

> 1

which is the remainder when 11 is divided by 2.

rerandom   **REPRODUCE RANDOM** e.g.,

The following sequence of inputs and outputs illustrate the primitive 'rerandom':

> random 100
> 95
> rerandom
> random 100
> 66
> rerandom
> random 100
> 66

The procedure 'rerandom' reseeds the random number generator with the same value so that the same sequence of pseudo-random integers can be reproduced.

round   **ROUND** e.g.,

> round 3.4

will output:

> 3

and:

> round 3.5

will output:

4

Similarly:

round −3.4

will output:

−3

and:

round −3.5

will output:

−4

sf   **SCREEN FACTS** e.g.,

sf

could output for example:

[1 TS 4 WINDOW 1]

The elements of the output List indicate:

> The background colour (black).
> The screen state (text screen).
> The number of text lines in the splitscreen's text window (4).
> The window state (whether there is a fence or not), (WINDOW, i.e. no fence).
> The graphic screen's aspect ratio (1).

shuffle   **SHUFFLE** e.g.,

To illustrate this primitive, we shall first assign a List of numbers to a variable called 'series':

make "series [1 2 3 4 5 6 7 8]
shuffle :series

could output for example:

[4 2 1 6 5 3 8 7]

that is, the elements of 'series' in random order. However, it should be noted that this does not change the order of the elements of the variable 'series', it only outputs them in a random order. This can be confirmed by entering:

                    :series

which will output:

                    [1 2 3 4 5 6 7 8]

sin   **SIN** e.g.,

                 sin 42

will output:

                    Ø.669130563735962

which is the sine of 42 degrees.

thing   **THING** e.g.,

                 thing "pig

will output:

                    bacon

It should be noted that 'thing' works rather like a colon in
that it outputs the value of the variable whose name follows
(preceded by double quotes), e.g.:

                    :pig

will also output:

                    bacon

However, as we shall see later, there are circumstances when
a colon cannot be used, and 'thing' becomes essential.

tf   **TURTLE FACTS** e.g.,

                 tf

will output a List whose elements contain information about
the Turtle, e.g.:

                    [Ø Ø Ø 15 PD TRUE]

The information contained in the six elements of the output
List are as follows:

                    X coordinate
                    Y coordinate
                    Heading

42

Pen colour
Pen up or Pen down or Pen erase
TRUE if the Turtle is visible, FALSE if the
Turtle is hidden

uc **UPPER CASE** e.g.,

uc "cat2

will output:

CAT2

where **WHERE** e.g.,
Will output the position of the last TRUE 'memberp' expression, e.g.:

memberp "rat [cat dog rat fish]
TRUE
where
3

which indicates that 'rat' was in position 3 in the List of which it is a member.

word **WORD** e.g.,

word "hill "side

will output:

hillside

However, if we were to enter for example:

word "hill "si "de

the computer would output:

hillsi
de

If we wish to make a single word out of more than two input words, then we must enclose the whole expression in parentheses, e.g.:

(word "hill "si "de)

will output:

hillside

43

wordp   **WORD PREDICATE** e.g.,

       wordp "pig

will output:

       TRUE

because 'pig' is a word. Similarly:

       wordp :pig

will output:

       TRUE

because the value of the variable 'pig' is a word ('bacon'). Moreover:

       wordp :angle

will also output:

       TRUE

because the value of the variable 'angle' i.e. '21' is also a word as well as being a number. However:

       wordp :insects

will output:

       FALSE

because the value of the variable 'insects' is the List '[flies beetles] ' rather than a simple word.

GRAPHICS

The graphics screens of BBCBASIC(Z80) and Dr.LOGO are
fundamentally different from each other. With BBCBASIC,
the origin (with coordinates 0,0) is in the bottom left-hand
corner of the screen. There are a total of 1024 X-coordinate
positions ranging from 0 to 1023, and a total of 768 Y-
coordinate positions ranging from 0 to 767. The coordinates
of the centre of the screen are thus approximately 512,384
as shown in Figure 1.

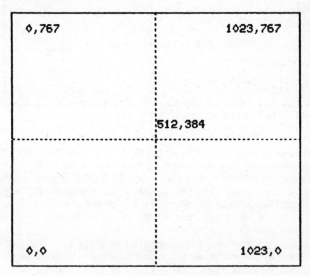

Fig.1   BBCBASIC(Z80) Graphics Screen

With Dr.LOGO, the origin is in the centre of the screen.
There are 254 different X-coordinate positions ranging from
−127 to +127, and there are 192 Y-coordinate positions
ranging from −96 to +96 as shown in Figure 2.
The graphics screen of the LOGO-Graphics Interpreter
presented at the end of the book has a coordinate layout
that is similar to Dr.LOGO in that the origin is in the centre
of the screen. However, there are 1024 X-coordinate

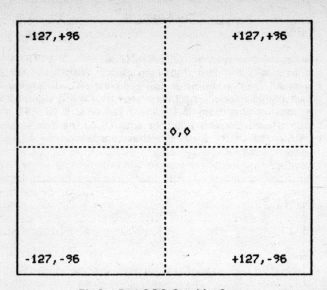

Fig.2   Dr.LOGO Graphics Screen

positions ranging from −512 to +512, and there are 660
Y-coordinate positions ranging from −330 to +330. Unlike
Dr.LOGO, there is a primitive in the LOGO-Graphics Interpreter called 'ORIGIN' which takes the parameter 'BL' which
resets the origin to the bottom left of the screen as in BBC-
BASIC, or 'MID' which resets the origin to the middle of the
screen as in Dr.LOGO.

It is possible to perform graphics operations in BBCBASIC
in immediate mode, although the graphics statements are not
really intended to be used in this way. It is usual to use the
graphics statements within BASIC programs. However, it is
useful to explore the graphics statements in immediate mode.

In LOGO on the other hand, the graphics procedures are
intended to be used in immediate mode. In fact, with a few
exceptions such as the definition of new procedures, most
work in LOGO is done in immediate mode. In LOGO, the
use of graphics procedures is quite straightforward, whereas
in BASIC, much more thought is required in advance.

In BASIC, all line drawing is done in relation to the cartesian coordinates of the start and the end of the line, these are

either the *absolute* coordinates, or coordinates *relative* to the last point plotted. There is an invisible graphics cursor that can be moved around the screen either drawing a line as it moves, or moving without drawing a line.

In LOGO, the Turtle takes the place of the graphics cursor, and can be either visible or invisible. If the Turtle is invisible, then the graphics operations are faster than if it is visible. This is because it takes a finite time to draw and undraw the Turtle each time it moves around the screen. As the Turtle moves around the screen, it can either place down on the screen, a notional 'pen', and draw a line as it moves, or it can lift the 'pen' off the screen, and move without drawing a line. The position and movements of the Turtle *can* be described in terms of cartesian coordinates. However, the movements of the Turtle are usually controlled by simple procedures such as 'FORWARD' ('fd'); 'RIGHT' ('rt'); 'LEFT' ('lt'); and 'BACK' ('bk'). The use of procedures such as these enables the Turtle to be 'driven' around the screen like a small vehicle.

We shall now consider the graphics facilities of BBCBASIC (Z80) and LOGO. The results will be given as screen-dumps to a printer. As the version of Dr.LOGO used here has no facility for printing out graphics screens, the LOGO graphics displays presented here are produced by the LOGO-Graphics Interpreter and dumped to the printer by a machine code routine. To draw a line of a given length with Dr.LOGO and with the LOGO-Graphics Interpreter, the same procedure names are used but all lengths used by the LOGO-Graphics Interpreter have to be 4 times as big as those used by Dr. LOGO. This is because the LOGO-Graphics Interpreter has 4 times the resolution of Dr.LOGO. Thus, for example, a line of 50 screen units in length in Dr.LOGO will be the same length as a line of 200 screen units in length in the LOGO-Graphics Interpreter. Similarly, a line of 50 screen units in Dr.LOGO is equivalent to a line of 200 screen units in BBCBASIC(Z80). Even though the LOGO graphics displays have been produced by the LOGO-Graphics Interpreter, the lengths quoted in the text will be those appropriate to Dr. LOGO.

A Simple Example: Drawing a Right-angled Triangle
The triangle shown in the screen display of Figure 3 can be produced in a number of ways with BASIC and with LOGO,

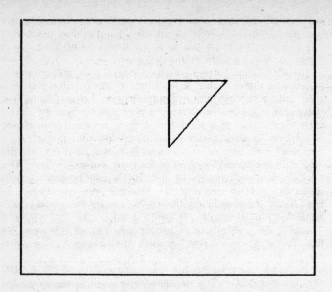

Fig.3 Screen Display

e.g.:

BASIC

```
CLS
MOVE 512,384
PLOT 1,0,200
PLOT 1,200,0
PLOT 1,-200,-200
```

will produce the display shown in Figure 3 as follows:

The 'CLS' statement clears the screen.

The 'MOVE' statement moves the invisible graphics cursor (without drawing a line) to the screen coordinates 512,384 (i.e. to the centre of the screen).

The first 'PLOT' statement draws a line in mode 1 (i.e. relative to the position of the graphics cursor) 0 units along the X axis, and 200 units along the Y axis. Thus, the first line to be drawn is the vertical line.

The second 'PLOT' statement draws a line in mode 1, 200 units along the X axis, and 0 units along the Y axis.

48

Thus, the second line to be drawn is the horizontal line, and the graphics cursor is now at the right-hand end of the line.

The third 'PLOT' statement draws a line in mode 1 (i.e. relative to the position of the graphics cursor), —200 units along the X axis, and —200 units along the Y axis, (i.e. back to where it started).

In general, in BBCBASIC(Z80), 'PLOT' statements take the following form:

PLOT mode-number,X coordinate,Y coordinate

where the mode-numbers cause the following actions:

Mode-number 0 moves the graphics cursor relative to its last position.

Mode-number 1 draws a line in the graphics foreground colour, relative to the last position of the graphics cursor.

Mode-number 3 draws a line in the graphics background colour, relative to the last position of the graphics cursor.

Mode-number 4 moves the graphics cursor to the absolute coordinates.

Mode-number 5 draws a line in the graphics foreground colour, to the absolute coordinates.

Mode-number 7 draws a line in the graphics background colour, to the absolute coordinates.

Mode-numbers 8 to 15 behave as modes 0 to 7, but the lines are drawn dotted.

Mode-numbers 16 to 23 behave as modes 0 to 7, but the lines are drawn dashed.

Mode-numbers 24 to 31 behave as modes 0 to 7, but the lines are drawn alternately dot-dashed.

Mode-number 37 draws an ellipse in the graphics foreground colour, centered on the position of the graphics cursor. The second and third parameters specify respectively the X and Y radii of the ellipse, (a circle can be drawn by making the X radius 3/4 the Y radius).

Mode-number 39 behaves like mode-number 37 but the ellipse is drawn in the graphics background colour.

Mode-numbers 45 and 47 behave like mode-numbers 37 and 39 respectively, but draw dotted lines.

Mode-numbers 53 and 55 behave like mode-numbers 37 and 39 respectively, but draw dashed lines.

Mode-numbers 61 and 63 behave like mode-numbers 37 and 39 respectively, but draw dot-dashed lines.

49

Mode-numbers 64 to 71 behave like mode-numbers Ø to 7, but plot a single point at the finishing position of the graphics cursor.

Mode-numbers 96 to 1Ø3 behave like mode-numbers Ø to 7, but fill in the area around the finishing position of the graphics cursor.

Mode-number −1 changes the graphics origin to the position specified by the second and third parameters.

An alternative way of drawing the right-angled triangle in BBCBASIC is to use the 'DRAW' statement, and to work out the absolute coordinates of the vertices of the triangle to which lines will be drawn, e.g.

```
CLS
MOVE 513,384
DRAW 512,584
DRAW 712,584
DRAW 512,384
```

The reader should try a third possibility of using absolute coordinates and 'PLOT' statements with the appropriate mode-numbers, as above.

LOGO

With LOGO it is possible, but it is not essential, to work with cartesian coordinates when one is drawing lines. Indeed, Turtle Graphics was designed to remove any such considerations from the process of line drawing, and to make line drawing a natural process in which it is possible to anthropomorphise the movements of the Turtle in terms of moving backwards and forwards, and of turning left and right. If the user does not actually know how to draw the required shape, then he/she can find out how to do it by experimentation. The following three short examples of LOGO use respectively, no coordinates, only coordinates, and a mixture of procedures that require, and others that do not require the use of cartesian coordinates:

```
cs
ht
fd 5Ø
rt 9Ø
```

```
        fd 50
        rt 135
        fd 70.71
```

The procedure 'cs' (CLEAR SCREEN) clears the graphics screen and places the Turtle in the centre of the screen (i.e. at the graphics origin with coordinates 0,0), and facing towards the top of the screen.

The procedure 'ht' (HIDE TURTLE) makes the Turtle invisible and thus speeds up any subsequent line drawing.

'fd 50' (FORWARD 50) causes the (invisible) Turtle to move forwards, i.e. in the direction it is facing, 50 screen units (which is equivalent to the 200 screen units of BBC-BASIC(Z80)), drawing a line as it goes. This therefore, draws the vertical line.

'rt 90' (RIGHT 90) causes the Turtle to turn right through 90 degrees so that now it is facing towards the right of the screen.

'fd 50' as before, causes the Turtle to move forwards 50 screen units, drawing a line as it goes. This therefore, draws the horizontal line.

'rt 135' causes the Turtle to turn right through 135 degrees in order to face the point from which it started. A knowledge of geometry would help here to get it right first time, but would not be essential. We have already drawn two sides of an isosceles triangle with an angle of 90 degrees at its apex. Therefore, because the internal angles of a triangle add up to 180 degrees, the two equal base angles must each be 45 degrees. It is now possible to deduce that the Turtle must be turned through 135 degrees in order to draw the base of the triangle (the diagonal line). This can either be deduced because this angle plus 45 must add up to 180 degrees, or because the exterior angle of a triangle is equal to the sum of the internal opposite angles, i.e. 90 + 45 = 135 degrees. However, a user who did not yet know that the Turtle must at this stage be turned through 135 degrees could experiment by turning the Turtle through experimental angles and drawing lines to see whether they pass through the correct point. Incorrect lines could be undrawn by using the procedure 'pe' (PEN ERASE) and going over them again. Experimentation in this way leads to empirical discovery.

'fd 70.71' causes the Turtle to move forwards a distance of 70.71 units back to the starting point. A knowledge of

Pythagoras would be needed to get this distance exactly right. It will be remembered that Pythagoras' Theorem states that the square of the hypotenuse is equal to the sum of the squares of the other two sides of a right angled triangle. If the length of the hypotenuse of the triangle = L, then:

$$L^2 = 50^2 + 50^2 .$$

Therefore:

$$L = (50^2 + 50^2)^{1/2} = 70.710678$$

Without a knowledge of Pythagoras, the triangle could still be completed by a process of experimentation. This would lead to a good empirical approximation to the length of the third side. Particularly with some guidance, the drawing of this triangle by this method could lead to an empirical discovery or demonstration of Pythagoras' Theorem. This is the experimental world of 'Mathland' where Seymore Papert would have children wander, making discoveries as they go. With the guidance of a teacher, and with the support of group discussion, Turtle graphics can form an integral part of a structured learning process which can complement periods of pure experimentation as favoured by Papert.

It is possible with Dr.LOGO to produce the same drawing of a right-angled triangle by using procedures that use cartesian coordinates, e.g.:

```
cs
ht
sety 50
setx 50
setpos [0 0]
```

The procedures 'cs' and 'ht' clear the graphics screen, place the Turtle at the origin, in the centre of the screen, and hide the Turtle as before.

'sety 50' moves the Turtle in the Y axis to Y coordinate 50, drawing a line as it goes. This therefore, draws the vertical line.

'setx 50' moves the Turtle in the X axis to X coordinate 50, drawing a line as it goes. This therefore, draws the horizontal line.

'setpos [0 0]' moves the Turtle to the coordinates specified by the List '[0 0]' i.e. back to the origin, drawing a line
as it goes.

Finally, we can use what is probably the easiest set of
commands to understand (as long as we remember that the
Turtle starts at the origin 0,0):

```
cs
ht
fd 50
rt 90
fd 50
setpos [0  0]
```

The procedures 'cs' and 'ht' behave as before.

'fd 50' moves the Turtle forward 50 screen units, drawing
a line as it goes, thus drawing the vertical line.

'rt 90' turns the Turtle to the right through 90 degrees.

'fd 50' moves the Turtle forward 50 screen units, drawing
a line as it goes, thus drawing the horizontal line.

Finally, 'setpos [0 0]' moves the Turtle back to the origin
(its starting position), drawing a line as it goes, thus complet-
ing the triangle.

In LOGO, it is possible to move the Turtle backwards (in
relation to the direction in which it is facing) by using the
procedure 'bk' ('BACK'), e.g.:

```
bk 50
```

will cause the Turtle to move backwards 50 screen units.
Whether the Turtle draws a line as it goes is determined by
whether the 'pen' is up or down.

The procedure 'pu' ('PEN UP') lifts the notional 'pen'
off the screen. While the 'pen' is up, the Turtle can move
around the screen without drawing any lines.

Changing Colour

In BBCBASIC and Dr.LOGO, it is possible to change the
colour of the background and the colour of the lines drawn.

In BBCBASIC(Z80) this is done by means of the 'GCOL'
statement which takes the form:

```
GCOL n1,n2
```

where 'n1' determines the backdrop colour. This is the colour of the border and of any areas which show through transparent sectors. The second parameter, 'n2' determines either the foreground or the background colour depending on its size. If n2 is greater than 127, then the background colour is determined. For example:

GCOL 4,11

sets the backdrop to dark blue, and the foreground, (i.e. any drawn lines) to light yellow. A second call to 'GCOL' as follows:

GCOL 4,128

would leave the backdrop and the foreground as defined by the previous 'GCOL' statement, but would set the background to transparent. Table 1 shows the colours that are produced by the various possible numbers:

Table 1
Colour-determining parameters in the 'GCOL' statement

Foreground	Background	Colour
0	128	Transparent
1	129	Black
2	130	Medium Green
3	131	Light Green
4	132	Dark Blue
5	133	Light Blue
6	134	Dark Red
7	135	Cyan
8	136	Medium Red
9	137	Light Red
10	138	Dark Yellow
11	139	Light Yellow
12	140	Dark Green
13	141	Magenta
14	142	Grey
15	143	White

In Dr.LOGO the colour of the background can be changed by means of the procedure 'setbg' ('SET BACKGROUND'), e.g.:

setbg 6

would set the background to dark red.

The colour of the Turtle, and any lines that it draws can be changed by means of the procedure 'setpc' ('SET PEN COLOUR'), e.g.:

setpc 11

will change the colour of the Turtle to light yellow. Any subsequent lines that are drawn by the Turtle will also be light yellow, until the pen colour is reset to another colour.

The parameters for the procedures 'setbg' and 'setpc' can range from Ø to 15 inclusive, and their corresponding colours are the same as those indicated for the foreground in Table 1.

PROGRAMS AND PROCEDURES

So far everything that we have done has been concerned with using BASIC and LOGO in immediate mode, i.e. one step at a time, rather like using a calculator. For example, if we wished to add 2 to 3, multiply the result by 4 and then print out the answer, we could enter:

BASIC

    PRINT(2+3)*4

LOGO

    pr (2+3)*4

Similarly, if we wish to calculate and print out the average of four numbers, we could for example, enter:

BASIC

    PRINT(3+5+7+12)/4

and the computer will print out:

    6.75 ,   or in LOGO:

LOGO

    pr (3+5+7+12)/4
    6.75

It would, however, be very tedious if all of these instructions had to be typed in every time the average of four numbers was required. Moreover, the tedium would be much worse if the calculations were at all lengthy.

The solution of course, is to produce a *program* in which the instructions are stored in sequence, so that they need only be typed in once, and thereafter only the data on which the program is to operate may have to be entered.

In BASIC a program is generated by typing in lines of statements (often with just one statement per line), each line is preceded by a line number. The computer will execute the program when the command 'RUN' is typed in. The BASIC interpreter will start at the lowest line number, execute the statement(s) on that line, and move on to the next highest line number, and so on until the whole program has been executed. Below is a simple BASIC program to compute the average of four numbers:

BASIC

```
100 INPUT A,B,C,D
110 PRINT(A+B+C+D)/4
120 END
```

In line '100', the computer waits for four numbers to be entered, separated by commas. In line '110', the arithmetic is performed and then the result is printed out. Line '120' is a non-essential line, and simply indicates that the program is at an end. In more complicated programs, the 'END' statement may be essential to prevent the interpreter from running on into sub programs that may reside at the highest line numbers. Once a BASIC program has been entered into the computer, it is executed when 'RUN' is typed in. Depending on the computer system in use, a program can be stored for future use on an auxiliary memory device such as a cassette tape, a continuous 'floppy tape', a 'floppy' discette, or a hard disc. When a program is required, it is loaded into the computer RAM from the auxiliary device such as a disc, and it is then available to be executed.

In LOGO the same task of computing the average of four numbers is approached in a different way. LOGO consists of a set of Primitives, i.e. Procedures that make up the basic building blocks of the language. When the name of any Procedure is entered, along with any required parameters, that Procedure is executed. If we wish to write a *program* in LOGO to compute the average of four numbers, then we have to define a new Procedure which LOGO will add to its dictionary of Procedures, and which, when its name is entered, along with any parameters, will compute the average of four numbers. This can be thought of as teaching the LOGO machine *to* compute an average of four numbers. It must always be remembered that there are many ways of solving even the simplest of problems, so that solutions to programming problems presented here are by no means unique. We shall define a rather crude Procedure to compute the average of four numbers in the first instance, but later, we shall refine it somewhat. However, before we actually define our new Procedure to compute the average, we shall look into the way new Procedures are defined.

57

Procedure Definition

In LOGO new Procedures are defined by using the Primitive 'to'. The word 'to' is followed by the name of the new Procedure, and any parameters. On subsequent lines, the bulk of the Procedure definition takes place, and the Procedure definition is terminated by the word 'end'. As an illustration, we shall define a Procedure called 'turn' that will simply cause the Turtle to draw a line 50 units long, turn right through 90 degrees, and draw another line 50 units in length:

LOGO

```
to turn
fd 50
rt 90
fd 50
end
```

It is possible to attach parameters to the definition of the Procedure, which will give it greater flexibility. For example, it would provide considerably more flexibility to the procedure 'turn' if we could pass to it a parameter to determine how far forward the Turtle is to move, instead of being restricted to the 50 units as in the example above. Similarly, it would provide more flexibility still if we could pass a parameter to 'turn' that would determine the angle through which the Turtle is to turn, instead of being restricted to 90 degrees as in the example above. This can be done easily as follows:

```
to turn :distance :angle
fd :distance
rt :angle
fd :distance
end
```

So for example, if we were to enter:

```
turn 20 45
```

the parameter 'distance' would take the value '20', and the parameter 'angle' would take the value '45'. This would thus cause the Turtle to move forward a distance of 20 screen units, turn right through 45 degrees, and move forward again

58

a distance of 2Ø screen units.

We shall now define a simple Procedure to compute the average of four numbers. As we learn more about LOGO, we shall define better, more flexible Procedures to compute averages.

LOGO

```
to enter
op first rl
end

to average1
make "a enter
make "b enter
make "c enter
make "d enter
op (:a+:b+:c+:d)/4
end
```

It can be seen that to begin with we have defined a small Procedure called 'enter'. This gives us a convenient way of entering numbers and is analagous to 'INPUT' in BASIC. 'READ QUOTE' ('rq') could be used, but it is not available in all versions of LOGO, whereas 'READ LIST' ('rl') is available in rather more versions. The Procedure 'enter' works as follows:

```
op first rl
```

Outputs the first element of an input List. We are in fact only going to enter a List containing a single element (our number). The Primitive 'rl' reads in the *contents* of a List, and automatically puts square brackets around the List. The Primitive 'first' returns the first element of its parameter which is the List returned by 'rl'. Therefore, 'enter' is synonymous with 'first rl'. Indeed, 'first rl' could have been used instead of 'enter' in the definition of the Procedure 'average1'. However, we have defined our own inputting Procedure 'enter' for three reasons: First, if it is to be used many times, it is more economical to write 'enter' than it is to write 'first rl'. Second, the meaning of 'enter' is more apparent than 'first rl' so the definition of the Procedure 'average1' becomes more readable. Third, we have demonstrated that Procedures, once defined, can be used in the definition of further Procedures.

If we wish to execute the Procedure 'average1', we simply type in its name. The procedure will stop for the inputting of four numbers, and will then output their mean. For example:

```
average1
2
4
7
8
5.25
```

We can see that 5.25 is the arithmetic mean of 2, 4, 7, and 8.

Programming in LOGO involves the construction of Procedures to do specific tasks. Each Procedure can be tested for correctness independently. Procedures can then be combined in the definition of further procedures still. The final LOGO program consists of a single Procedure that will execute when its name is entered. As LOGO programming is naturally modular, LOGO favours a structured method of programming that involves the development of program modules, and the practice of *top down* program design.

With top-down program design, the programmer first of all starts with an idea of what the program is to achieve. For example, the program could be to draw a simple house. So, the name of the Procedure that will draw the house could be 'house :size' for example, where ':size' is a parameter that will determine how large the drawing of the house will be.

The next stage is to split the program into separate manageable modules, each of which will do a clearly defined job, and which can be tested independently. For example, the drawing of the simple house could be divided into the drawing of the roof in red, and then the walls in white. The names of the Procedures to do these tasks could be for example, 'roof :length' and 'walls :height' where ':length' and ':height' are parameters that control the lengths of the lines drawn by the Procedures 'roof' and 'walls' respectively.

The definition of the Procedure 'house' can now start to take shape, e.g.:

```
to house :size
roof :size
walls :size
end
```

It will now be necessary to define the procedures 'roof' and 'walls' before the procedure 'house' can be executed. However, when they have been defined, it will be possible to test them independently of each other.

Whilst in LOGO it is natural to develop programs in a modular way, in BASIC, modular programming is less obvious, and there can be a tendency to develop large monolithic programs that have little structure. It is however, good programming practice with BASIC to develop programs that consist of segments of code, each segment having a particular job to perform. A program of any consequence should be broken into subroutines which perform particular tasks, and a main program which calls the appropriate subroutines in the correct order.

BBCBASIC is a modern BASIC with Procedures. The Procedures of BBCBASIC are somewhat similar to Pascal Procedures, and are substantially more powerful than normal BASIC subroutines. In fact, the Procedures of BBCBASIC render the normal subroutines virtually redundant. The features that make BBCBASIC Procedures more powerful subprograms than regular BASIC subroutines are as follows:

1. Procedures are called by name rather than by line number as in most subroutines.

2. Procedures can contain local variables that are 'known' only to the Procedure, and will not affect the value of variables with the same name elsewhere in the program.

3. Procedures can have parameters passed to them. In BBCBASIC the parameters are restricted to simple variables, and cannot include structured types such as arrays as is possible in Pascal.

We shall define a simple procedure in BBCBASIC to draw a square anywhere on the screen, and of any size:

BASIC

```
100 CLS
110 PROC_SQUARE(512,384,200)
120 PROC_SQUARE(100,200,50)
130 END
140 DEF PROC_SQUARE(X,Y,L)
150 MOVE X,Y
160 DRAW X+L,Y
170 DRAW X+L,Y-L
180 DRAW X,Y-L
190 DRAW X,Y
200 ENDPROC
```

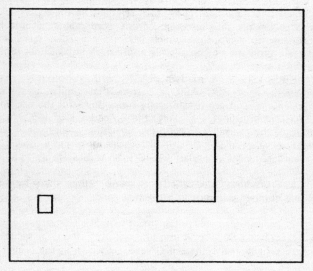

Figure 4

The BBCBASIC program consists of two distinct parts. Lines 100–130 are the main program, and lines 140–200 constitute the definition of the Procedure 'SQUARE', which is a subprogram. The job of the main program is to call the Procedure 'SQUARE' twice, and to pass different parameters to it on each occasion. The results of executing the program are shown in Figure 4.

Line 140 starts the definition of the Procedure 'SQUARE', and in brackets are listed the *formal parameters* of the Procedure. Lines 110 and 120 each call the Procedure 'SQUARE', and in brackets are listed the *actual parameters* that are to be passed to 'SQUARE'. Thus, for example, the call to 'SQUARE' on line 110 passed 512 to the parameter 'X'; 384 to the parameter 'Y'; and 200 to the parameter 'L'. This causes the Procedure to draw a square with its top left-hand corner situated at coordinates 512,384, and with sides of length 200 screen units. This is the largest of the two squares drawn in Figure 4. Similarly, the call to 'SQUARE' on line 120 passes 100 to the parameter 'X'; 200 to the parameter 'Y'; and 50 to the parameter 'L'. This causes the Procedure 'SQUARE' to draw the smaller square, with sides of length 50 screen units, and with the top left-hand corner of the square situated at coordinates 100,200.

User-defined Functions
We have already seen that there are present in BBCBASIC a large number of Standard Library Functions. It is possible however, to define subprograms called *User-defined Functions* that will return a single value when they are executed. User-defined Functions are similar to Procedures in a way, however, as we have seen. Procedures do not necessarily return a single value as their result. In the Procedure 'SQUARE' no values were returned as results, but rather, a square was drawn on the screen. User-defined Functions in BBCBASIC share the same three features that were listed above for Procedures. As an example, we shall define a single line Function called 'GEOM' that will return the geometric mean of two numbers:

BASIC
```
100 INPUT A,B
110 PRINT GEOM(A,B)
120 END
130 DEF FN_GEOM(X,Y)=SQR(X*Y)
```

The definition of the Function 'GEOM' is made on line 130. It can be seen that 'GEOM' has two formal parameters, 'X' and 'Y'. When the Function 'GEOM' is called on line 110, the actual parameters 'A' and 'B' are passed to the Function and 'X' and 'Y' take on the values of 'A' and 'B' respectively.

Global Variables and Local Variables

In both LOGO and BBCBASIC, variables can be of two types, *global* and *local*. Global variables are 'known' to all of the program, and can be changed by any of the segments of the program. Local variables on the other hand, are only 'known' to the Procedure (or Function) in which they are declared, and they do not affect the values of any global variables which may have the same names. For example:

BASIC

```
100 SWM=50
110 PROC_DISPLAY
120 PRINT SWM
130 END
140 DEF PROC_DISPLAY
150 LOCAL SWM
160 SWM=100
170 PRINT SWM
180 ENDPROC
```

On line 100, the global variable 'SWM' is set to 50, and on line 120 its value is printed out. Line 110 calls the Procedure 'DISPLAY' which is defined between lines 140 and 180 inclusive. The Procedure 'DISPLAY' declares a local variable 'SWM' (note that this is the same name as the global variable 'SWM'). Line 160 sets the local variable 'SWM' to 100, and line 170 prints out its value. Thus, when the program is executed, the computer will print out:

```
100
50
```

This demonstrates that even though the local variable 'SWM' was set to 100, it did not affect the value of the global variable 'SWM' which had previously been assigned the value of 50.

LOGO also has global variables and also local variables which are only 'known' to the procedure in which they are declared or any calling procedures. Consider the following LOGO session. The prompt '?' is the regular LOGO prompt, and the prompt '>' is the prompt given by LOGO during a Procedure definition. If there is no prompt shown, then this is a line output by the computer:

LOGO

```
?make "swm 100
?to display :swm
>pr :swm
>end
display defined
?display 50
50
?pr :swm
100
```

The first line assigns the value '100' to a global variable 'swm'. Then a Procedure called 'display' is declared that requires a parameter 'swm'. Parameters of Procedures are in fact, local variables. The only thing that the Procedure 'display' does is to print out the value of 'swm', its parameter. Thus, when 'display 50' is entered, the computer prints out '50'. However, subsequently, and outside the Procedure 'display', the command 'pr :swm' will cause the value of the global variable 'swm', i.e. '100' to be printed out.

As with BBCBASIC, it is possible in Dr.LOGO to declare variables to be local within Procedure definitions. Consider the following LOGO sessions:

LOGO

```
?make "swm 100
?to display2
>local "swm
>make "swm 40
>pr :swm
>end
display2 defined
?display2
40
?pr :swm
100
```

It can be seen that the value of the global variable 'swm' is not affected by the assignment of '40' to the local variable 'swm'. When the command 'display2' is entered, then the Procedure of that name is executed and the computer prints out '40', the value of the local variable 'swm'. However, when the command 'pr :swm' is entered, the computer prints out

'100', the value of the global variable 'swm'.

Local variables are also accessible to calling Procedures as the following LOGO session demonstrates. It is assumed that the global variable 'swm' has been assigned the value '100', and that the Procedure 'display2' has already been defined as above:

LOGO

```
?to display3
>pr :swm
>display2
>end
display3 defined
?display3
100
40
```

The Procedure 'display3' first of all prints out the value of the global variable 'swm', and then itself calls the Procedure 'display2' which prints out the value of the local variable 'swm'.

Comments

Comments are sections of code within a program that are not executed by the BASIC, LOGO or other language translator. They are included to make the program more readable. This is particularly important for the maintenance of the program (i.e. making changes to the program. These changes could be to eliminate bugs, or to change the function of the program in some way, e.g. changing V.A.T. rates in a business program).

In BASIC, comments are preceded by the word 'REM'. When the BASIC interpreter comes across a 'REM', then that line is ignored, e.g.:

BASIC

```
100  REM PROGRAM TO SQUARE A NUMBER
110  INPUT A
120  PRINT A*A
130  END
```

In LOGO, comments are proceded by a semi-colon, e.g.:

LOGO

```
to square :n
; procedure to square a number
op :n * :n
end
```

Recursion

Recursion occurs when a subprogram calls itself. A very simple example of a recursive subroutine call is given below in BASIC:

BASIC

```
100  REM SIMPLE RECURSIVE CALL
110  X=0
120  GOSUB 150
130  END
140  REM SUBROUTINE THAT CALLS ITSELF
150  X=X+1
160  PRINT X;
170  GOSUB 150
180  RETURN
```

In many versions of BASIC, subroutine 150 would call itself a limited number of times, and then the program would stop with an error message. For example, SHARP SP-5025 BASIC will allow the subroutine to call itself 16 times and then will stop with a GOSUB error at line 170. This happens because this particular interpreter will only allow subroutines to nest 16 deep. BBCBASIC(Z80) however, will allow the subroutine to call itself indefinately. However, the example given above only shows a simple feature of recursion, i.e. that a subprogram calls itself. With true recursion, each recursive call causes new copies of any variables used to be created. Thus for example, it is possible for a variable called 'REK' for the sake of argument, to exist on each level of the recursion process. In other words, there will be as many separate variables called 'REK' as there have been recursive calls, and they will all exist at the same time. BBCBASIC (Z80) is fully recursive, and this can be demonstrated by a recursive Function definition to compute the factorial of a number. (For example, factorial 5 = 5*4*3*2*1, and by definition, factorial 0 = 1).):

BASIC

```
100 REM RECURSIVE FACTORIAL FUNCTION
110 INPUT A
120 PRINT FN_FACT(A)
130 GOTO 110
140 DEF FN_FACT(N)
150 IF N=0 THEN =1
160 =N*FN_FACT(N-1)
```

LOGO is also fully recursive as can be seen by the following recursive definition of a procedure to compute the factorial of a number:

LOGO

```
to fact :n
if :n = 0 [op 1]
op :n * fact :n - 1
end
```

In both the BASIC and the LOGO examples above, we have used an 'if-then' conditional branch. This type of control structure is discussed in the next section.

Control Structures

Computer programs consist of instructions that determine the sequence of processes that will produce the desired result. In BASIC, the processes are determined by statements that are located at particular line numbers. The computer will execute statements in order of their line numbers or in order of their position within a line unless instructions are met that divert the sequence of execution to another part of the program. *Control* is said to reside in the statement currently being executed. Thus, control flows from one statement to the next in the order specified by the program. There are various ways of manipulating the flow of control through a program. The program structures that effect the various flows of control are called 'control structures'. In LOGO, within Procedure definitions, control flows from one line of the definition to the next in a way similar to the flow of control in a BASIC program.

Linear Sequence

The simplest control structure is the linear sequence, where control flows from one line to the next, and is not diverted, e.g.:

BASIC

```
100  REM LINEAR SEQUENCE
110  INPUT A
120  B=INT(A)*2
130  PRINT B
140  END
```

LOGO

```
to inter  :a
;  linear sequence
make "b 2 * int :a
pr  :b
end
```

With the segment of BASIC code, and the LOGO Procedure, the linear sequence is obvious. A value is entered, a variable 'B' or 'b' is assigned the value of twice the integer part of the input value, and its value is then printed out.

IF-THEN Conditional Branching

Flowchart 1 shows an IF-THEN conditional branch in which the flow of control is diverted according to the result of a test. The example is as follows:

A number is entered. If it is greater than 10, then the computer will print out a message that the number is greater than 10, and will then print out the word 'finished'. The following programs illustrate this type of control structure:

BASIC

```
100  REM IF-THEN CONDITIONAL BRANCH
110  INPUT X
120  IF X>10 THEN PRINT"GREATER THAN
       10"
130  PRINT"FINISHED"
140  END
```

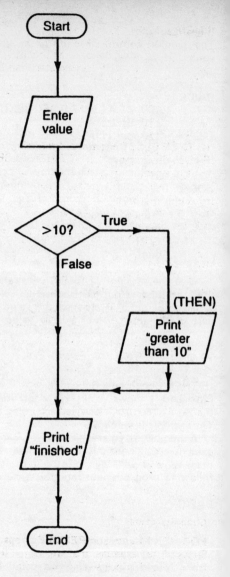

Flowchart 1

70

LOGO

```
to branch1 :x
; if-then conditional branch
if (:x > 10) [pr [greater than 10] ]
pr [finished]
end
```

IF-THEN-ELSE Conditional Branching

Flowchart 2 shows an IF-THEN-ELSE conditional branch control structure in which the flow of control is diverted down one of two possible paths, depending on the result of a test. A number is entered; if it is greater than 10 then 'Greater than 10' is printed out followed by 'Finished'. If the entered number is not greater than 10, then 'Not greater than 10' is printed out followed by 'Finished'.

BASIC

```
100  REM IF-THEN-ELSE CONDITIONAL
     BRANCH
110  INPUT X
120  IF X>10 THEN PRINT"GREATER THAN
     10" ELSE PRINT"NOT GREATER THAN
     10"
130  PRINT"FINISHED"
140  END
```

LOGO

```
to branch2 :x
; if-then-else conditional branch
if (:x > 10) [pr [greater than 10] ] [pr [not greater
     than 10] ]
pr [finished]
end
```

Loop Structures

FOR-NEXT Loops and REPEAT Loops

Suppose, for example, that we wished to print out the integers from 1 to 10 inclusive. This could be done in BASIC as follows:

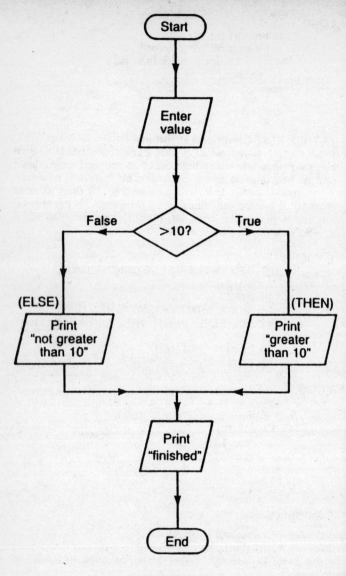

Flowchart 2

BASIC

```
100  REM FOR-NEXT LOOP
110  FOR I=1 TO 10
120     PRINT I
130  NEXT I
140  END
```

In this structure, the variable 'I' is called a *control variable*. The control variable 'I' is incremented by 1 each time the statements between the 'FOR' and the 'NEXT' statements are executed. It should be noted that the statement(s) between the 'FOR' and the 'NEXT' have been indented in the program listing. Indenting the source text in this way serves to highlight the structure, and thus makes the code more readable. The same structure is shown below as a 'repeat' loop in LOGO:

LOGO

```
to loop
make "i 0
repeat 10 [make "i :i + 1 pr :i]
end
```

Note that the variable 'i' is initialised to zero at the start. Then the procedures within the square brackets are executed 10 times, with the variable 'i' being incremented and then printed out with each cycle of the loop.

Looping with Steps

Suppose that we wished to write a program similar to the For-Next loop example above, but that we wished to print out every other integer, starting with '1' and stopping when the integer becomes greater than '9'. In a BASIC FOR-NEXT loop, it is possible to use a 'STEP' parameter which will determine by how much the control variable is incremented after each cycle of the loop. For example:

BASIC

```
100  REM FOR-NEXT-STEP LOOP
110  FOR I=1 TO 10 STEP 2
120     PRINT I
130  NEXT I
140  END
```

This will cause the control variable 'I' to be incremented by '2' with each cycle of the loop. When this program is executed, the computer will print out the numbers: 1,3,5,7,9. Note that although the control variable is specified to range from '1' to 10' in steps of '2', when 'I' has a value of '9' and is incremented by '2', 'I' now has a value of '11' which is greater than the upper limit of the control variable of '10', so the interpreter exits from the loop. The same structure can be created in LOGO as shown below:

LOGO

```
to steploop
; looping in steps of 2
make "control_variable 1
label "start
    pr :control_variable
    make "control_variable :control_variable + 2
if (:control_variable < 10) [go "start]
end
```

We can see that the loop structure is created by using a label 'start' as a destination for a 'go' command which is part of a conditional branch. It is possible to loop with negative steps, and this is illustrated below in LOGO:

LOGO

```
to negloop
; looping with negative steps
make "cv 10
label "start
    pr :cv
    make "cv :cv - 1
if (:cv > -11) [go "start]
end
```

Leaving Loops Early

It is sometimes necessary to exit a loop before the control variable has reached its limit value. This would usually be the result of a condition being fulfilled during the execution of the loop. In BBCBASIC(Z80), if control is diverted out of a FOR-NEXT loop, the FOR address is left on the Stack because the control variable has not reached its limit value.

74

This will give rise to problems which can be avoided simply by setting the control variable to 1 greater (assuming positive STEP values) than the limit value immediately before leaving the loop. For example:

BASIC

```
100 REM LEAVING A LOOP EARLY
110 INPUT X
120 FOR I=1 TO 10
130    X=X*2
140    PRINT I,X
150    IF X>500 THEN I=11
160 NEXT I
170 PRINT"FINISHED"
180 END
```

Nesting FOR-NEXT or REPEAT Loops
BASIC FOR-NEXT or LOGO REPEAT loops can be nested as illustrated by the following examples:

BASIC

```
100 REM NESTING FOR-NEXT LOOPS
110 FOR I=1 TO 3
120    FOR J=1 TO 2
130       PRINT I
140       PRINT J
150    NEXT J
160 NEXT I
170 END
```

A LOGO procedure equivalent to the above BASIC program is given below:

LOGO

```
to nest
; nesting repeat loops
make "i 0
repeat 3 [make "i :i + 1 make "j 0 repeat 2 [make
    "j :j + 1 pr :i pr :j ] ]
end
```

75

Both of the above examples would produce the following output:

```
                1
                1
                1
                2
                2
                1
                2
                2
                3
                1
                3
                2
```

REPEAT-UNTIL Loops

It is often required that a block of statements or Procedures be repeatedly executed *until* a certain condition becomes true. This type of structure can be represented by Flowchart 3.

It can be seen from the flow diagram that in the REPEAT-UNTIL control structure, the statement block is always executed at least once. This is illustrated by the following program:

BASIC

```
100 REM REPEAT-UNTIL LOOP
110 INPUT X
120 REPEAT
130     X=X*2
140     PRINT X
150 UNTIL X>=100
160 PRINT"FINISHED"
170 END
```

The statements on lines 130 and 140 will repeatedly execute until the value of the variable 'X' becomes equal to, or greater than 100; in which case, the word 'FINISHED' is printed out. For example:

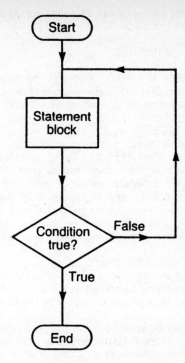

Flowchart 3

If '2' is entered, then the computer will print out:

        4
        8
        16
        32
        64
        128
FINISHED

If '50' is entered, then the computer will print out:

        100
FINISHED

If '200' is entered, then the computer will print out:

400
FINISHED

A REPEAT-UNTIL loop can be constructed in LOGO. It is important to distinguish between a LOGO REPEAT loop, (which is the equivalent of a BASIC FOR-NEXT loop), and a REPEAT-UNTIL loop. The two loop structures do have fundamentally different purposes. The REPEAT, or FOR-NEXT loop is intended to execute a fixed number of times. The REPEAT-UNTIL loop however, is intended to execute at least once, and to continue executing until a pre-defined condition becomes true. The example is given below in LOGO, and it can be seen that the loop is constructed by means of a conditional branch that tests for the condition that will determine whether an exit is made from the loop, *after* the statement block within the loop.

LOGO

```
to until :x
; repeat-until loop
label "start
    make "x :x * 2
    pr :x
if (:x < 100) [go "start]
pr [finished]
end
```

The output from the LOGO procedure 'until' is exactly the same as that from the BASIC REPEAT-UNTIL loop above.

WHILE Loops
Some versions of BASIC directly support WHILE loops which have the following format:

```
WHILE (logical expression)
    //STATEMENT BLOCK//
ENDWHILE (or WEND)
```

Strangely, BBCBASIC does not directly support WHILE loops, so it is necessary to construct them as it also is in LOGO. This type of control structure is represented by Flowchart 4.

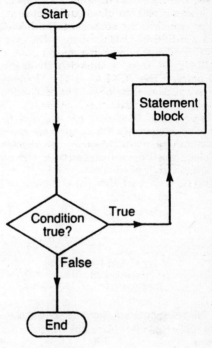

Flowchart 4

It can be seen from Flowchart 4 that in the WHILE loop, the statement block within the loop need not ever be executed. This is the essential difference between a REPEAT-UNTIL loop (where the statement block within the loop is always executed at least once) and a WHILE loop. This is because the condition that is tested to determine whether an exit is to be made from the loop, is tested *before* the statement block within the loop with a WHILE loop, and *after* the statement block with a REPEAT-UNTIL loop.

A WHILE loop is illustrated by the following program:

BASIC

```
100 REM WHILE LOOP
110 INPUT X
120 REM WHILE X<=100
130 FOR I=1 TO 2 STEP 0
140     IF X>100 THEN I=3:GOTO 180
150     X=X*2
160     PRINT X
170     REM ENDWHILE
180 NEXT I
190 PRINT"FINISHED"
200 END
```

The statements on lines 150 and 160 will repeatedly execute *while* the value of the variable 'X' is less than or equal to 100; in which case, the word 'FINISHED' is printed out. For example:

If '2' is entered, then the computer will print out:

```
                4
                8
               16
               32
               64
              128
    FINISHED
```

If '50' is entered, then the computer will print out:

```
              100
              200
    FINISHED
```

If '200' is entered, then the computer will print out:

```
    FINISHED
```

The reader should compare the results produced by the WHILE loop and the REPEAT-UNTIL loop, and should try to understand them in terms of the flow of control within the different loop structures.

It should be noted that the way we constructed the WHILE loop in BBCBASIC was to use a FOR-NEXT loop with a STEP parameter of zero. This is in fact a REPEAT-FOREVER loop. On line 140 within the Repeat-Forever loop, the condition is tested to determine whether to exit the loop. In this case, whether the value of the variable 'X' is greater than 100. When this condition becomes true, the value of the control variable 'I' is set to 3 (i.e. one greater than the limit value of 2), and control is transferred to line 180 by a 'GOTO' statement. On line 180, the interpreter finds that the value of 'I' is greater than 2 and so control exits from the loop, and the word 'FINISHED' is printed out.

The same program is defined below as a LOGO procedure called 'while':

LOGO

```
to while :x
; while loop
label "start
if (:x > 100) [go "exit]
    make "x :x * 2
    pr :x
go "start
label "exit
pr [finished]
end
```

The output from the LOGO procedure 'while' is exactly the same as that from the BASIC WHILE-loop program above.

REPEAT-FOREVER Loops

It is sometimes desirable to make the computer execute a never-ending loop. Below are given simple examples that will repeatedly print out the word 'FOREVER' until the machine is turned off, or until one breaks into the program, for example, by pressing the 'ESC' key.

BASIC

```
100  REM REPEAT FOREVER LOOP
110  PRINT"FOREVER"
120  GOTO 110
```

or if one wishes to avoid a backward 'GOTO' which can slow down a program if there are many program lines before the start of the loop:

BASIC

```
100  REM REPEAT FOREVER LOOP
110  FOR I=1 TO 2 STEP 0
120      PRINT"FOREVER"
130  NEXT I
```

The same structure is given below in LOGO:

LOGO

```
to forever
label "start
     pr [forever]
go "start
end
```

Extending LOGO

We have already been extending LOGO each time we have defined a new Procedure.

Different implementations of LOGO are provided with various Procedures that are the LOGO equivalents of Standard Library Functions, and we have already seen those available in the Z80 Dr.LOGO used here. There are however, several important Functions that are not provided. However, as LOGO is an extensible language, it is possible to define Procedures to provide these missing Functions.

In this section we shall define a number of Procedures to provide a variety of mathematical Functions, some of them familiar to the BASIC programmer, and others not available in BASIC. Moreover, we shall also define Procedures that will effectively create the structured data types, arrays, with both one and two dimensions; and we shall define new Procedures for the handling of these arrays.

We shall define our new Procedures in a modular fashion, with some Procedures performing intermediate tasks in the definitions of other Procedures even though some of them may be directly useable Procedures in their own right. Our first example is in this category, this is the Procedure 'power':

Definition of 'power'
The Procedure 'power' will raise a value 'x' to an integer power 'p'.

```
to power :x :p
local "v
make 'v 1
repeat :p [make "v :v * :x]
op :v
end
```

Thus, if we enter 'power 3 2', the computer will raise 3 to the power 2, and print out '9'.

Definition of 'In'
The Procedure 'In' is intended to be purely an intermediate Procedure, in that it will be used by other Procedures, but is not intended to be used directly. In fact, 'In' will compute the natural logarithm of a number between −1 and 1. It will be used by other Procedures that will compute logarithms to the base 1Ø, and natural logarithms of any number. This Procedure depends on the convergent logarithmic series:
If we wish to compute the natural log of 'a', then:

$$a=(1+x)/(1-x)$$

and

$$x=((a-1)/(a+1))$$

in the series:

$$1/2\log.((1+x)/(1-x))=x+x^3/3+x^5/5+x^7/7+...$$

```
to In :a
(local "b "l "cycle)
make "b (:a − 1) / (:a + 1)
make "l :b
make "cycle 1
label "loop
    make "cycle :cycle + 2
    make "l :l + (power :b :cycle) / :cycle
    if :cycle = 25 [make "l :l * 2 op :l]
go "loop
end
```

83

This will compute the first 25 terms of the series. This is a slow Procedure. It can be speeded up by computing fewer terms in the series, with a reduction in accuracy.

Definition of 'log'

The Procedure 'log' will compute the logarithm to the base 1Ø of any number. It works by moving the decimal point to the left until the number is less than 1 (whilst keeping count of the number of shifts to the left made by the decimal point. This count is called 'div'). Then, the Procedure 'ln' is called to compute the natural log of the number which is less than 1. The result is then divided by 2.3Ø25851, which is the natural log of 1Ø. Then the value of 'div' is added. The result is output.

```
to log :x
(local "div "ll)
make "div −1
label "start
    make "div :div + 1
    if :x < 1 [make "ll (ln :x) / 2.3Ø25851
        + :div op :ll]
go "start
end
```

Definition of 'exp'

The Procedure 'exp' will compute e^x for any value of 'x'. The Procedure 'exp' uses the power series:

$$e^x = 1 + 1/1! + x^2/2! + x^3/3! + \ldots + x^r/r! + \ldots$$

This is an infinite series which converges to a limit for every finite value of 'x'. The Procedure 'exp' computes the sum of the first 12 terms of the series.

```
to exp :x
(local "ex "cycle)
make "ex :x + 1
make "cycle 1
repeat 12 [make "cycle :cycle + 1 make "ex
        (:ex + (power :x :cycle) / (fact :cycle))]
op :ex
end
```

Note that this Procedure makes calls to the Procedures 'power' and 'fact' which have both been defined earlier, and which respectively compute the integer power, and the factorial of an input value.

Definition of 'antilog'
The Procedure 'antilog' will output the antilog of a $\log_{10}$ value:

```
to antilog :x
local "anti
make "anti :x * 2.3025851
make "anti exp :anti
op :anti
end
```

It can be seen that the Procedure 'antilog' makes a call to the Procedure 'exp'. The reader may notice that it would be quite possible to replace the third and fourth lines in the definition of 'antilog' by a single line. I have used two lines simply to facilitate readability.

Definition of 'loge'
The Procedure 'loge' will output the natural logarithm of any number:

```
to loge :x
op 2.3025851 * (log :x)
end
```


Definition of 'sqr'
The Procedure 'sqr' is intended to be used as an intermediate Procedure that will be used by a subsequently defined Procedure called 'sqrt'. The Procedure 'sqr' takes three parameters which we shall call 'n', 'low', and 'hi'. The value 'n' is the number whose square-root is required, 'low' is a value lower than the square-root, and 'hi' is a value higher than the square-root. The Procedure works by making an estimate of the square-root by taking the mean of 'low' and 'hi'. This quantity is called 'av'. The value 'av' is squared and subtracted

from 'n'. The result of this subtraction is called 'dif'. If 'dif' exactly equals zero, then clearly the square-root of 'n' has been found. However, this is an unlikely event and so a level of accuracy (the tolerance) has to be chosen. In the case here, we choose a tolerance of 10^{-4}. That is, if the value of 'dif' is less than 10^{-4}, then we consider that the square-root has been found. However, if the square of 'av' is greater than 'n' then 'hi' is set to the value of 'av' else, 'low' is set to the value of 'av'. The Procedure 'sqr' is then recursively called. Eventually the estimate of the square-root of 'n' is output:

```
to sqr :n :low :hi
(local "ss "dif "av)
make "av (:low + :hi) / 2
make "ss :av * :av
make "dif :ss — :n
if :dif < Ø [make "dif — :dif]
if :dif < 1.e—Ø4 [op :av]
if :ss = :n [op :av]
if (:ss > :n) [op sqr :n :low :av]
             [op sqr :n :av :hi]
end
```

Definition of 'sqrt'
The Procedure 'sqrt' outputs the square-root of an input value. This Procedure calls the Procedure 'sqr', and passes to it 'n', '1' as 'low', and 'n' as 'hi'. The reader may like to improve this procedure by outputting an error message if a negative number is entered:

```
to sqrt :n
op sqr :n 1 :n
end
```

Definition of 'npr'
The Procedure 'npr' computes permutations. This is a Function not available in BASIC. This Procedure takes two inputs 'n' and 'r', and outputs ^nP_r, i.e. the number of permutations of r objects taken from n different objects. The Procedure uses the relationship:

$$^nP_r = n!/((n-r)!)$$

```
to npr :n :r
(local "num "denom)
make "num fact :n
make "denom fact (:n — :r)
op :num / :denom
end
```

Definition of 'ncr'

A group of r objects with no regard to the order of arrangement is called a *combination*. The Procedure 'ncr' takes two inputs, 'n' and 'r', and outputs the value of ^nC_r, the number of combinations of r objects taken from n different objects. The Procedure uses the following relationship:

$$^nC_r = n!/((n-r)!r!)$$

```
to ncr :n :r
(local "num "denom)
make "num fact :n
make "denom (fact (:n — :r)) * (fact :r)
op :num / :denom
end
```

This also is a Function that is not available in BASIC.

Definition of 'raise'

The Procedure 'raise' is rather like the Procedure 'power' in that it raises a number to a given power, however, 'raise' can raise a number to a fractional power, whereas, 'power' can only raise a number to an integer power.

```
to raise :x :y
op antilog ((log :x) * :y)
end
```

For example:

raise 3   2.5

will output:

15.5884383003095

which is $3^{2.5}$ accurate to 4 decimal places.

Definition of 'swap'
The Procedure 'swap' takes two inputs, 'x' and 'y', and swaps
their values:

```
to swap :x :y
local "temp
make "temp thing :x
make :x thing :y
make :y :temp
end
```

Implementing Arrays in LOGO
We have seen that LOGO supports simple variables, and that
the *type* of the variable is determined by what is being done
with the variable at the moment. LOGO also makes considerable use of Lists, and has powerful List-processing facilities.
It is possible however, to effectively implement arrays in
LOGO by using the Procedure 'word'. The Procedure 'word'
works by taking two input words and concatenating them into
a single word. If the name of the array is the first word, and
a number is the second word, then the Procedure 'word' will
concatenate these two objects to form the name of another
object that could be a variable name, e.g.:

```
make word "matrix 2   42
```

will concatenate 'matrix' and '2' to form 'matrix2', and will
assign the value of 42 to the variable called 'matrix2'. The
following would do the same thing:

```
make word "matrix "2   42
```

If we enter:

```
pr :matrix2
```

the computer will print out:

42

The numeric part of the variable name thus created, e.g. the '2' in 'matrix2' could be used to represent a location in an array called 'matrix'. Below is the definition of a Procedure called 'dim' which behaves rather like 'DIM' in BASIC, and initialises an array to zero:

Definition of 'dim'

```
to dim :array :lim
local "loc
make "loc Ø
repeat :lim [make "loc :loc + 1 make word :array
      :loc Ø]
end
```

Thus for example, if we enter:

dim "matrix 5

an array called 'matrix' will be set up containing five elements, and each element will have the value of zero. Actually the variables:

matrix1
matrix2
matrix3
matrix4
matrix5

will all be assigned the value of zero.

We shall now define a Procedure call 'inparr' which will allow us to input the values into a named array:

Definition of 'inparr'

```
to inparr :array :lim
(local "temp "loc)
```

89

```
make "loc Ø
repeat :lim [make "loc :loc + 1 make "temp
       word :array :loc pr word "Enter_
       :temp make word :array :loc
       first rl]
end
```

Below is an example of a session using the Procedure
'inparr':

```
?inparr "matrix 2
Enter_matrix1
42
Enter_matrix2
42.24
?
```

The first line, 'inparr "matrix 2' specifies that the first two
elements of the array called 'matrix' are to be entered. A
prompt is given before each value is entered. If one then
enters for example:

pr :matrix1

the computer will print out:

42

If we enter:

pr :matrix3

the computer will print out:

Ø

because the variable 'matrix3' was initialised to zero by the
previous 'dim' Procedure.

We shall now define a Procedure called 'disparr' that will
print out the first n values in an array:

Definition of 'disparr'

```
to disparr :array :lim
local "loc
make "loc Ø
repeat :lim [make "loc :loc + 1
      pr thing word :array :loc]
end
```

Below is an example of a session using the Procedure 'disparr':

```
?disparr "matrix 5
42
42.24
Ø
Ø
Ø
?
```

The computer thus printed out the first 5 elements of the array 'matrix'.

The part of the definition of 'disparr' which prints out the values is, 'pr thing word :array :loc'. We can see that 'loc' is incremented with each execution of the repeat loop and will thus successively take the values 1,2,3,4,5. The part, ':array' is the name of the array, in this case 'matrix' and the current value of 'loc', e.g. 'matrix2' when 'loc'=2. Finally, 'thing' returns the value of e.g. 'matrix2', and 'pr' prints it out.

Two-dimensional Arrays

We have just seen that it is possible to implement one-dimensional arrays in LOGO. It is possible to implement two-dimensional arrays by correctly indexing the elements of a suitably sized one-dimensional array.

If we have an array with r rows and c columns, then it is clear that a one-dimensional array of size r*c will be exactly the correct size to hold all of the values to be stored in the r by c array.

If we wish to index the element 'table(i,j)' in the array 'table' which has r rows and c columns, then if we actually set

up a one-dimensional array called 'table' of size r*c as follows,
(let r=2, and c=3):

```
dim "table 6
```

then the element 'table(i,j)' can be indexed as 'table(c*(i−1)
+j)'.

We shall define a Procedure called 'matdim' that will
declare a two-dimensional array, and assign zeroes to each of
the elements of the array:

Definition of 'matdim'

```
to matdim :array :ci :cj
local "lim1
make "lim1 :ci * :cj
make word "id :array :cj
dim :array :lim1
end
```

For example:

```
matdim "table 2 3
```

will declare a two-dimensional array called 'table' to have 2
rows and 3 columns, and will initialise all of the elements of
the array to $\emptyset$. In fact, what happens is that a one-dimensional
array called 'table' is set up to have 2*3=6 elements. We can
see that this is done by calling the Procedure 'dim', and passing
r*c as its numeric parameter. However, the line:

```
make word "id :array :cj
```

sets up another variable called in this case 'idtable', and
assigns to it the number of columns required in the two-
dimensional array 'table'. This variable is required by other
Procedures yet to be defined, that will access the various
elements of the two-dimensional array.

We shall now define a Procedure called 'matfind'. The
function of 'matfind' is to locate a particular element within
a named two-dimensional array. It should be noted that the
Procedure 'matfind' makes use of the variable 'id*arrayname*'
which contains the number of columns in the named two-

dimensional array. It should also be noted that it uses the algorithm for indexing the (i,j)[th] element described previously.

Definition of 'matfind'

```
to matfind :array :ci :cj
local "temp
make "temp thing word "id :array
make "lok (:temp * (:ci − 1) + cj)
end
```

The Procedure 'matfind' assigns to the global variable 'lok' the location of the (i,j)[th] element of the two-dimensional array within the one-dimensional array in which it is implemented.

We shall now define a Procedure called 'matput' which enables us to enter a quantity into a given element of a named two-dimensional array:

Definition of 'matput'

```
to matput :array :ci :cj :quant
matfind :array :ci :cj
make word :array :lok :quant
end
```

For example, if we enter:

matput "table 2 2 42

the element in the second row, second column of the two-dimensional array 'table' will be assigned the value 42.

We shall now define a Procedure called 'matpr' that will output the value of a given element in a named two-dimensional array.

Definition of 'matpr'

```
to matpr :array :ci :cj
matfind :array :ci :cj
op thing word :array :lok
end
```

For example, if we enter:

matpr "table 2 2

the Procedure will output '42', assuming 42 had been entered into this particular element for example, by 'matput' as above.

A Sorting Procedure

It is frequently the case that we wish to sort numbers that are stored in an array. We shall define here a Procedure called 'sort' that will sort the first n numbers in a named array into ascending order. We shall use the simplest of sorting algorithms called bubblesort. In this version of bubblesort, each array location is taken in turn, and the value stored at that location is compared with all of the values stored at higher locations. If the value at the higher location is smaller than the value at the lower location, then they swap places. The result of this is that after the first pass along the array, the smallest value is in the lowest array position. After the second pass, the second smallest value is in the second array position, etc. A total of n−1 passes are needed to sort an array containing n values.

We shall first present a segment of BASIC code that will bubblesort an array called 'A( )', and then give the LOGO equivalent:

BASIC

```
100  REM THERE ARE N VALUES IN
     THE ARRAY A( )
110  REM BUBBLESORT SEGMENT
120  FOR I=1 TO N−1
130    FOR J=I+1 TO N
140      IF A(I)>A(J) THEN TEMP=A(I):
         A(I)=A(J):A(J)=TEMP
150    NEXT J
160  NEXT I
170  REM  END  OF  BUBBLESORT  SEGMENT
```

LOGO Definition of 'sort'

```
to sort :array :lim
; bubblesort
```

```
(local "i "j)
make "i Ø
make "j Ø
label "istart
make "i :i + 1
make "j :i
label "jstart
make "j :j + 1
if ((thing word :array :i) > (thing word :array
      :j)) [swap word :array :i word :array :j]
if :j < :lim [go "jstart]
if :i < :lim − 1 [go "istart]
end
```

We shall now illustrate the ease of program development in LOGO once we have extended the LOGO vocabulary of Procedures to include functions that are suitable for our own particular applications. We shall develop a program to read n values into a named array, sort the values, and then print out the sorted values. We shall call the Procedure 'order'.

Definition of 'order'

```
to order :array :lim
inparr :array :lim
sort :array :lim
pr [Sorted values]
disparr :array :lim
end
```

Below is an example of a session using the Procedure 'order':

```
?order "mat 4
Enter_mat1
42
Enter_mat2
42.24
Enter_mat3
15
Enter_mat4
21
Sorted values
```

95

```
15
21
42
42.24
?
```
.

The program (Procedure) 'order' would have been quite a large object if it had been written in BASIC. However, it was quite a simple job to develop it in LOGO. This is because all of the component Procedures had been previously defined, and reside in the LOGO workspace as part of the vocabulary of LOGO. Each Procedure is available for incorporation into the definition of other Procedures. This illustrates the fundamental difference between the methods of program development in BASIC and in LOGO. Program development in LOGO takes place by the defining and testing of named Procedures which effectively become part of the LOGO language. The closest that we can get to this with BASIC is to save collections (libraries) of Subroutines or Procedures on tape or disc, and then to incorporate them into new programs as required. This is only possible if the version of BASIC being used has a 'MERGE' facility, and is greatly facilitated if it also has a 'RENUMBER' command.

We shall end this section by defining another Procedure called 'mean', to compute the average of a set of numbers. However, this time the numbers will reside in a named array. The Procedure 'mean' will output the mean of the first *lim* numbers in the named array:

```
to mean :array :lim
(local "total "loc)
make "total Ø
make "loc Ø
repeat :lim [make "loc :loc + 1
             make "total :total +
             thing word :array :loc]
op :total / :lim
end
```

An example session using the Procedure 'mean' follows:

```
?mean ''mat 4
30.06
?
```

where 30.06 is the mean of the first 4 numbers in the array 'mat'.

It would be a simple matter to define a new Procedure called e.g. 'summary' which combines the processing of the Procedures 'order' and 'mean', as follows:

```
to summary :name :number
order :name :number
pr mean :name :number
end
```

The reader should work out exactly what the Procedure 'summary' will do.

GRAPHICS PROGRAMMING

We have already considered the various graphics statements and Procedures in BBCBASIC and LOGO, and the layouts of the BASIC and LOGO graphics screens. However, we have only considered simple graphics in immediate mode.

Whilst it is quite natural to use LOGO in immediate mode for graphics applications (in fact, Turtle-Graphics is specifically designed to facilitate immediate mode graphics operations), BASIC is definitely not designed for immediate mode graphics. For any complex graphics applications, it is necessary to write program, or to define Procedures which will do the various tasks associated with the production of a sophisticated graphical display.

We shall begin our graphics programming with three simple examples of LOGO code that produce complex and interesting displays by repeating a simple set of operations a number of times with a partial rotation between each set of operations. The Turtle finishes in the same position exactly that it starts. Such operations are called 'state-transparent' because the state of the Turtle remains unaltered after the operations are complete.

The first state-transparent Procedure that we shall define is called 'star'. This Procedure works by drawing 12 squares, and rotating the Turtle through 30 degrees after each square is drawn:

LOGO
```
to star
repeat 12[repeat 4[fd 40 lt 90] lt 30]
end
```

Figure 5 shows the result of entering 'star' once it has been defined as above. The result is an interesting pattern that forms a twelve-pointed star.

A slightly more complex design can be produced by the Procedure 'diamond'. This Procedure produces a display which resembles the facets on a cut gemstone, as shown in Figure 6. Once again, this Procedure is state-transparent:

LOGO
```
to diamond
repeat 10[rt 36 repeat 5[fd 40 rt 72]]
end
```

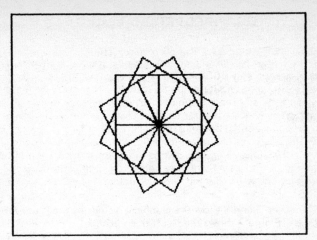

Fig.5   Display produced by the Procedure 'star'

It should be remembered that in every case, the LOGO graphics display will be drawn much quicker if the Turtle is first 'hidden' by using the Procedure 'ht' (HIDE-TURTLE).   This is because when it is hidden, the Turtle does not have to be drawn and undrawn every time it moves.

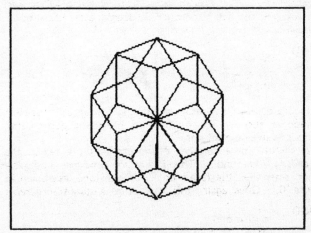

Fig.6   Display produced by the Procedure 'diamond'

We shall now define a Procedure called 'flags' that takes an input parameter. In this Procedure, the Turtle draws a shape that resembles a flag on a stick. The Turtle then moves to a position part way along the 'stick' and turns right through 30 degrees. The parameter of 'flags' specifies how many flags will be drawn in this way:

LOGO

```
to flags  :number
ht
repeat  :number [fd 40 repeat 4[fd 20
                        rt 90] bk 25 rt 30]
end
```

Figures 7 and 8 show the graphical output of the Procedure 'flags'. Figure 7 shows the result of entering:

flags 3

and Figure 8 shows the result of entering:

flags 12

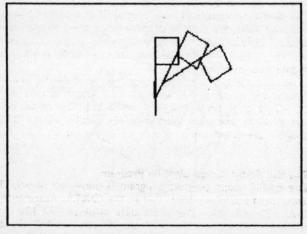

Fig.7   Displays produced by the Procedure 'flags'

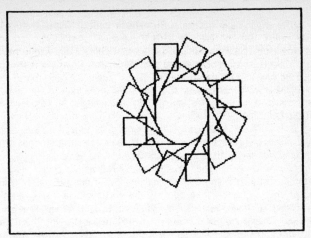

Fig.8   Displays produced by the Procedure 'flags'

Graph Plotting

We shall now present BBCBASIC and LOGO programs to plot normal X,Y graphs. The graphs will plot the data points as square symbols, and join them with straight lines. The axes will be labelled and scaled to the largest X and Y values. The BASIC program will only plot positive values of X and Y, and will have the option of drawing a grid on the screen display. The LOGO program will have its origin in the centre of the screen, and will be able to plot both positive and negative values of X and Y.

As a project, the reader should write a BASIC program which will produce the same kind of screen display as the LOGO program presented here, and a LOGO program which will produce the same kind of screen display as the BASIC program presented here.

The BBCBASIC Graph-plotting Program

The BASIC graph plotting program is presented below. The data for plotting are contained in the 'DATA' statements on lines 120 and 140. The single data value on line 120 is the number of data points (in this case 6). On line 140, the data point coordinates are present as consecutive X,Y values.

Lines 180 to 200 determine whether a grid will be drawn or not, and specify the labels for the X and Y axes.

Lines 240 to 260 read in the coordinates of the data points (an 'INPUT' statement could be used here to allow data to be entered at run time).

Lines 280 to 350 sort the X values into ascending order, and carry the Y values with their associated X values. A simple bubblesort is used.

Lines 370 to 410 find the maximum X and Y values, and lines 430 to 470 scale the values to their maxima so that the graph will exactly fit the graph space.

Line 480 calls the Procedure 'FRAME' which resides between lines 740 and 920 inclusive. The Procedure 'FRAME' begins by setting the graphics screen to white on a black background (line 750). Line 760 tests to find whether a grid is to be drawn or not. If a grid is not to be drawn, then the grid lines are made very short and just appear as short marks on the axes. If a grid is to be drawn, then the grid lines are made long so that they stretch across the graph space. Lines 790 to 830 draw the surround frame of the graph space, lines 840 to 870 draw the vertical grid lines, and lines 880 to 910 draw the horizontal grid lines.

Lines 490 to 610 draw the data points as squares and join them up with straight lines.

Lines 630 to 720 label the axes, and the program ends on line 730.

Figures 9 and 10 show the graphical output of this program. Figure 9 shows the graph with a grid drawn, and Figure 10 shows the graph without a grid.

```
100 REM GRAPH PLOTTING PROGRAM
110 REM NUMBER OF DATA POINTS
120 DATA 6
130 REM X,Y,X ETC.
140 DATA 1,0.5,2,3,4.5,3.5,6,7.5,
7,6.5,9.5,10.24
150 CLS
160 PRINT"ENTER G FOR A GRID"
```

```
  170 PRINT"OR PRESS ENTER FOR NO G
RID"
  180 INPUT GRID$
  190 X$="X AXIS"
  200 L$="Y AXIS"
  210 READ N
  220 DIM X(N),Y(N),P(N),Q(N)
  230 REM READ DATA COORDINATES
  240 FOR I=1 TO N
  250    READ X(I),Y(I)
  260 NEXT I
  270 REM SORT X AND CARRY Y
  280 FOR I=1 TO N-1
  290    FOR J=I+1 TO N
  300       IF X(J)>=X(I) THEN 340
  310       TEMP=X(I):T=Y(I)
  320       X(I)=X(J):Y(I)=Y(J)
  330       X(J)=TEMP:Y(J)=T
  340    NEXT J
  350 NEXT I
  360 REM FIND MAXIMUM Y VALUE
  370 YM=-0.000001
  380 FOR I=1 TO N
  390    IF Y(I)>YM THEN YM=Y(I)
  400 NEXT I
  410 XM=X(N):REM MAXIMUM X VALUE
  420 REM SCALE VALUES
  430 KX=700/XM:KY=600/YM
  440 FOR I=1 TO N
  450    P(I)=X(I)*KX
  460    Q(I)=Y(I)*KY
  470 NEXT I
  480 PROC_FRAME
  490 MOVE P(1)+300,Q(1)+100
  500 FOR I=1 TO N
  510    P(I)=P(I)+300
```

103

```
520     Q(I)=Q(I)+100
530     REM JOIN POINTS
540     DRAW P(I),Q(I)
550     REM DRAW POINTS AS SQUARES
560     MOVE P(I)-10,Q(I)-10
570     DRAW P(I)+10,Q(I)-10
580     DRAW P(I)+10,Q(I)+10
590     DRAW P(I)-10,Q(I)+10
600     DRAW P(I)-10,Q(I)-10
610 NEXT I
620 REM LABEL AXES
630 PRINT TAB(5,2);YM
640 PRINT TAB(6,20);"0.00"
650 PRINT TAB(12,21);"0.0"
660 PRINT TAB(37,21);XM
670 PRINT TAB(21,21);X$
680 LOC=6
690 FOR I=1 TO LEN(L$)
700     PRINT TAB(9,LOC);MID$(L$,I,
1)
710     LOC=LOC+1
720 NEXT I
730 END
740 DEFPROC_FRAME
750 GCOL 129,15
760 IF GRID$="G" THEN VERT=700:HO
RI=1000:GOTO 780
770 VERT=110:HORI=310
780 CLS
790 MOVE 300,100
800 DRAW 1000,100
810 DRAW 1000,700
820 DRAW 300,700
830 DRAW 300,100
840 FOR I=300 TO 1000 STEP 70
850     MOVE I,100
```

104

```
860    DRAW I,VERT
870 NEXT I
880 FOR I=100 TO 700 STEP 60
890    MOVE 300,I
900    DRAW HORI,I
910 NEXT I
920 ENDPROC
```

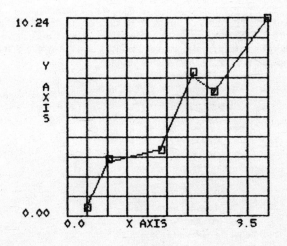

Figure 9

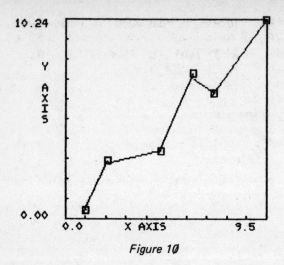

Figure 10

Dr.LOGO Graph-plotting Procedure

The Procedure 'plot' will be defined below. It will take three parameters. The first two parameters are the names of the arrays that contain the X and Y values respectively, and the third parameter is the number of data points to be plotted. It will be seen that 'plot' calls four other user defined Procedures called 'scale', 'axes', 'point', and 'printat'. These Procedures will be defined in due course:

LOGO

```
to plot :arr1 :arr2 :lim
ht
(local "index "x "y)
scale :arr1 :arr2 :lim
axes
pu
make "index 1
make "x thing word "sx "1
make "y thing word "sy "1
setpos list :x :y
point :x :y
pd
repeat :lim − 1 [make "index :index + 1
```

106

```
            make  "x thing word "sx  :index make  "y
            thing word "sy :index setpos list :x
            :y point :x :y]
    printat 10  12 [X axis]
    printat 22  17 [Y axis]
    printat 20  12  "0
    printat 18  4  :ymax
    printat 17  18 —:ymax
    printat 36  12  :xmax
    printat  1  12 —:xmax
    end
```

The Procedures called by 'plot' are defined below, together
with Procedures that they call:

```
    to scale :arr1 :arr2 :lim
    local "loc
    make  "loc 0
    repeat :lim [make "loc :loc + 1 make
        word "sx :loc thing word
        :arr1 :loc make word "sy
        :loc thing word :arr2 :loc]
    make  "xmax max :arr1 :lim
    make  "ymax max :arr2 :lim
    make  "scx 120 / :xmax
    make  "scy 60 / :ymax
    make  "loc 0
    repeat :lim [make "loc :loc + 1 make
        word "sx :loc (thing word
        "sx :loc) * :scx make word
        "sy :loc (thing word "sy :loc)
        * (:scy)]
    end
```

The Procedure 'scale' scales the individual X and Y values
to their maxima. This Procedure calls the additional Procedure 'max' which outputs the maximum value in a named
array. The Procedure 'max' is defined below:

```
    to max :arr :limit
    local "pos
    make  "pos 0
    make  "va "
```

107

```
repeat :limit [make "pos :pos + 1 make
    "va se thing word :arr
    :pos :va]
make "hi −1.e−Ø3
high :va
op :hi
end
```

The Procedure 'max' makes a further call to a recursive Procedure called 'high' which is defined below:

```
to high :xxx
if emptyp :xxx [stop]
if first :xxx > :hi [make "hi first :xxx]
high bf .xxx
end
```

The Procedure 'plot' next calls a Procedure called 'axes' which draws a box around the graph space and draws the axes. The Procedure 'axes' is defined below:

```
to axes
frame
pu
setpos [−12Ø Ø]
rt 9Ø
pd
repeat 24 [lt 9Ø fd 2 bk 2 rt 9Ø fd 1Ø]
lt 9Ø
fd 2
pu
setpos [Ø −6Ø]
pd
repeat 12 [lt 9Ø fd 2 bk 2 rt 9Ø fd 1Ø]
lt 9Ø
fd 2
pu
end
```

The Procedure 'axes' calls a Procedure called 'frame'. The Procedure 'frame' draws the box around the graph space:

108

```
to frame
setscrunch 1
cs
pu
setpos [−127 64]
pd
setpos [127 64]
setpos [127 −64]
setpos [−127 −64]
setpos [−127 64]
end
```

The next Procedure called by 'plot' is called 'point'. This Procedure takes two parameters which are the X and Y co-ordinates of a data point, and plots the point as a square symbol at the appropriate screen position:

```
to point :x :y
pu
setpos list :x − 1 :y + 1
pd
setpos list :x + 1 :y + 1
setpos list :x + 1 :y − 1
setpos list :x − 1 :y − 1
setpos list :x − 1 :y + 1
pu
setpos list :x :y
end
```

The last Procedure to be called by 'plot' is called 'printat'. The Procedure 'printat' takes three parameters. The first two parameters are text-screen coordinates which specify the row and the column in which text is to be printed. The third parameter is the text that is to be printed at the specified screen position:

```
to printat :x :y :wd
ct
setcursor list :x :y
pr :wd
ct
end
```

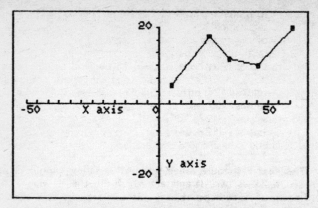

Fig.11   Display produced by the Procedure 'plot'

Figure 11 gives an example of the graphic output of the Procedure 'plot'. An example of a call to the Procedure 'plot' is given below.

    ?plot "x "y 5

where 'x' is the name of an array containing the values to be used as X values, and 'y' is the name of an array containing the values to be used as Y values. The '5' specifies that the first 5 elements in each of the two specified arrays are to be used for plotting.

THE LOGO-GRAPHICS INTERPRETER

The LOGO-Graphics Interpreter is written in BBCBASIC (Z80) and the source code is given at the end of the book. Lines 1010 and 1020 are specific to the Einstein computer and serve to create the square brackets necessary for LOGO. Lines 7970 and above are extra to the basic graphics interpreter.

The syntax of the interpreter is very similar to that of Dr.LOGO but there are some differences:

1. The first difference is that everything is in upper case.

2. In either immediate mode, or in Procedure definitions, only one command per line is allowed. This is no disadvantage, and actually makes for more readable text.

3. The Procedure-editor 'ED ''procedurename' is more primitive than the Dr.LOGO editor, and only allows specified lines to be replaced.

4. The Procedure 'SETPOS' takes two parameters as in Dr. LOGO, but they are not contained within square brackets as they would be in Dr.LOGO, e.g.:

    SETPOS 30 50

It would be quite possible for the reader to change the Interpreter so that the square brackets would be required if this were considered to be desirable.

5. The Procedure 'OP' is quite different from 'op' in Dr. LOGO. In the Interpreter, 'OP' means display the value of the specified numeric variable on the screen, e.g.:

    OP :universe

6. The Interpreter is not recursive, so recursive Procedure definitions will not work.

7. The Procedure 'FILL' has been provided which fills the area around the Turtle with the current pen colour. It

should be noted that the 'ink' will 'leak' out through any holes in the outline of a shape being filled. To avoid this, it is advisable to work with a hidden Turtle.

8. All of the arithmetic functions that are available to BBC-BASIC are also available to the Interpreter, e.g. LOG(X). Therefore, they will not be presented as separate functions below in the description of the LOGO-Graphics Interpreter. All arithmetic expressions should be enclosed in brackets, e.g. MAKE "X (2*:Y).

The LOGO-Graphics Interpreter Primitives
The following Primitive Procedures are included in the LOGO-Graphics Interpreter. They are presented as specific examples, i.e. including example parameters where appropriate:

BK 50

BYE   (returns to BASIC)

CLEAN

CS

CT

ED "procedurename :X   (calls up the Editor to edit the Procedure called 'procedurename' that also takes the parameter 'X')

END

FD 100

FILL

HOME

HT

LT 45

112

```
MAKE "X 50          or:
MAKE "X :Y

OP :X

PD

PE

PO "TRIANGLE       or:
PO "TRIANGLE :SIDE

PONS

POTS

PU

PR [text to be printed]

REPEAT 3           or:
REPEAT :N          REPEAT loops can be
                   nested 2 deep

[

]                  The square brackets are
                   used to delimit 'REPEAT'
                   loops

RQ

RT 90

SETPC 3            Will set the pen colour to
                   green

SETPOS 50 100

ST

SETX 50
```

SETY 100

TO TRIANGLE   or:
TO TRIANGLE :SIDE

Extra Procedures

CIRCLE 50

Will draw a circle of radius 50 around the current position of the Turtle.

DASHED

Causes all subsequent lines drawn to be dashed lines.

DOTTED

Causes all subsequent lines drawn to be dotted lines.

FILE FRED

Causes all user-defined Procedures to be saved under the filename 'FRED'.

LOAD FRED

Causes the file of user-defined Procedures saved under the name 'FRED' to be loaded. These Procedures are not available for editing or examination by the Procedure 'PO'.

ORIGIN MID

Will set the Graphics origin to the middle of the screen; or:

ORIGIN BL

Will set the Graphics origin to the bottom left of the screen.

SOLID

Will cause all subsequent lines drawn to be solid.

STOPIF (:A<:B)

Stops the execution of the current Procedure if the logical expression is true.

Example Procedure Definitions with the Interpreter
We shall use the Interpreter to define the Procedures 'DIAMOND' and 'FLAGS' that we have previously defined in

114

Dr.LOGO. We shall also define a Procedure called 'PIC' that draws a defined number of randomly placed filled in circles of random diameters, and of random colour. This is a Procedure that cannot be defined directly in Dr.LOGO:

```
TO DIAMOND
REPEAT 10
[
RT 36
REPEAT 5
[
FD 150
RT 72
]
]
END


TO FLAGS :NUMBER
HT
REPEAT :NUMBER
[
FD 150
REPEAT 4
[
FD 80
RT 90
]
BK 100
RT 30
]
END


TO PIC :N
ORIGIN BL
REPEAT :N
[
MAKE "X (RND(1)*1000)
MAKE "Y (RND(1)*600)
PU
SETPOS :X :Y
MAKE "R (RND(1)*150)
```

```
MAKE "C (RND(1)*15)
SETPC :C
PD
CIRCLE :R
FILL
]
END
```

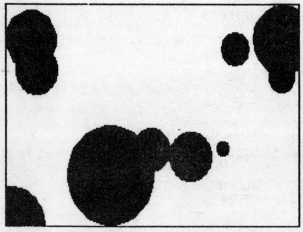

Fig.12   Display produced by the Procedure 'PIC'

Source-code of the LOGO-Graphics Interpreter
The source-code for the LOGO-Graphics Interpreter follows.
The Interpreter as presented here is written in BBCBASIC
(Z80), and was written on a Tatung Einstein computer.
Very little work should be involved in implementing this
Interpreter on a BBC microcomputer. The major constraint
here will be available memory depending on the machine
being used. It should not be too difficult to implement the
interpreter on other machines which do not support BBC-
BASIC, but of course, more work will be required.

116

```
>LIST
 1000 CLS:GCOL 129,15
 1010 *CHAR 91,0,112,64,64,64,64,11
2,0
 1020 *CHAR 93,0,28,4,4,4,4,28,0
 1030 ON ERROR GOTO 8150
 1040 COLOUR 9
 1050 PRINT TAB(17,8);"TURTLE"
 1060 COLOUR 11
 1070 PRINT TAB(8,10);"LOGO GRAPHIC
S INTERPRETER"
 1080 COLOUR 7
 1090 PRINT TAB(10,12);"BY S.J.WAIN
WRIGHT 1987"
 1100 COLOUR 15
 1110 FOR I=1 TO 5000:NEXT I
 1120 REM THIS PROGRAM MAY ONLY BE
TYPED INTO, STORED BY AND EXECUTED
ON A COMPUTER FOR USE BY THE OWNER
OF THIS BOOK.
 1130 REM THE LOANING OF COPIES OF
THIS PROGRAM OR THE SALE OF COPIES
OF THIS PROGRAM HOWEVER STORED, IS
NOT PERMITTED.
 1140 CLS
 1150 DIM R$(50),S$(50),P$(50),Q$(5
0),NAME$(50),NAM$(50),W$(50),S(50),
E(50),PR$(50),PA$(50),WA$(50),RR$(5
0),SS$(50),PP$(50),QQ$(50),RRR$(50)
,SSS$(50),PPP$(50),QQQ$(50)
 1160 X=512:Y=335:CURRENT=90:ANGLE=
90:TEMP=0:XX=0:YY=0:PU=0:THETA=0:PE
N=5:HT=0:VARNUM=0:WO=0:DD=0:FLAG0=0
:FLAG1=0:FLAG2=0:COORX=512:COORY=33
5
```

117

```
1170 PROC_FRAME
1180 MOVE X,Y
1190 PROC_TURTLE
1200 PROC_COMMAND
1210 PROC_ANALYSE(A$)
1220 PROC_DO(PRO$,PAR$)
1230 GOTO 1200
1240 END
1250 DEF PROC_COMMAND
1260 CL$="                                        "
1270 REM CL$ HAS 40 SPACES BETWEEN
THE QUOTES
1280 INPUT LINE TAB(0,0);A$
1290 PRINT TAB(0,0);CL$
1300 PRINT TAB(0,1);CL$
1310 ENDPROC
1320 DEF PROC_FRAME
1330 GCOL 129,11
1340 MOVE 0,0
1350 DRAW 1023,0
1360 DRAW 1023,670
1370 DRAW 0,670
1380 DRAW 0,0
1390 GCOL 129,15
1400 ENDPROC
1410 DEF PROC_ANALYSE(AA$)
1420 LOCAL I
1430 PRO$="":PAR$=""
1440 I=0
1450 I=I+1
1460 BIT$=MID$(AA$,I,1)
1470 IF BIT$=" " THEN 1510
1480 PRO$=PRO$+BIT$
1490 IF I=LEN(AA$) THEN ENDPROC
```

118

```
1500 GOTO 1450
1510 I=I+1
1520 BIT$=MID$(AA$,I,1)
1530 PAR$=PAR$+BIT$
1540 IF I=LEN(AA$) THEN ENDPROC
1550 GOTO 1510
1560 DEF PROC_DO(W$,N$)
1570 WORD$=W$:NUM$=N$
1580 PROC_FILE
1590 IF W$="FILE" THEN ENDPROC
1600 PROC_LOADD
1610 IF W$="LOAD" THEN ENDPROC
1620 LEVEL=0:GOTO 8170
1630 IF W$="STOPIF" THEN 2100
1640 PROC_ORIGIN
1650 IF W$="ORIGIN" THEN 2100
1660 PROC_CT
1670 PROC_PR
1680 PROC_PO
1690 IF W$="PO" THEN 2100
1700 PROC_ED
1710 IF W$="ED" THEN 2100
1720 IF WORD$="BYE" THEN CLS:PRINT
"BASIC":END
1730 PROC_TO
1740 PROC_MAKE
1750 IF W$="MAKE" THEN ENDPROC
1760 PROC_OP
1770 IF W$="OP" THEN ENDPROC
1780 PROC_UNTURTLE
1790 PROC_SETPOS
1800 IF W$="SETPOS" THEN 2100
1810 IF NUM$="" THEN NUM$="1"
1820 PROC_VARCHECK
1830 PAR=EVAL(NUM$)
```

119

```
1840 PROC_SETY
1850 PROC_SETX
1860 PROC_SETPC
1870 PROC_REPEET
1880 PROC_FD(PEN)
1890 REM BK MUST COME AFTER FD
1900 PROC_BK
1910 REM RT MUST COME BEFORE LT
1920 PROC_RT
1930 PROC_LT
1940 PROC_CS
1950 PROC_PU
1960 PROC_PD
1970 PROC_HT
1980 PROC_ST
1990 PROC_PE
2000 PROC_DASHED
2010 PROC_DOTTED
2020 PROC_SOLID
2030 PROC_CIRCLE
2040 PROC_PONS
2050 PROC_POTS
2060 PROC_FILL
2070 PROC_HOME
2080 PROC_CLEAN
2090 PROC_LEVEL1(WORD$,NUM$)
2100 PROC_TURTLE
2110 ENDPROC
2120 DEF PROC_FD(MD)
2130 IF WORD$<>"FD" THEN ENDPROC
2140 L=PAR
2150 YY=SIN RAD(ANGLE)*L
2160 XX=COS RAD(ANGLE)*L
2170 XT=XX+X:YT=YY+Y
```

```
 2180 IF PU=1 THEN MOVE XT,YT:GOTO
2200
 2190 PLOT MD,XT,YT
 2200 X=XT:Y=YT
 2210 ENDPROC
 2220 DEF PROC_LT
 2230 IF WORD$<>"LT" THEN ENDPROC
 2240 THETA=PAR
 2250 YT=Y+YY:XT=X+XX
 2260 ANGLE=THETA+CURRENT
 2270 CURRENT=ANGLE
 2280 TEMP=ANGLE
 2290 XT=X+XX:YT=Y+YY
 2300 WORD$="FD":PAR=5
 2310 PROC_FD(PEN)
 2320 WORD$="BK"
 2330 PROC_BK
 2340 ENDPROC
 2350 DEF PROC_RT
 2360 IF WORD$<>"RT" THEN ENDPROC
 2370 WORD$="LT"
 2380 PAR=-PAR
 2390 ENDPROC
 2400 DEF PROC_BK
 2410 IF WORD$<>"BK" THEN ENDPROC
 2420 PAR=-PAR:WORD$="FD"
 2430 PROC_FD(PEN)
 2440 ENDPROC
 2450 DEF PROC_TURTLE
 2460 IF HT=1 THEN ENDPROC
 2470 PLOT 37,15,20
 2480 ENDPROC
 2490 DEF PROC_UNTURTLE
 2500 IF HT=1 THEN ENDPROC
 2510 PLOT 39,15,20
```

```
 2520 ENDPROC
 2530 DEF PROC_CS
 2540 IF WORD$<>"CS" THEN ENDPROC
 2550 X=512:Y=335:CURRENT=90:ANGLE=
90:TEMP=0:XX=0:YY=0:PU=0:THETA=0:PE
N=5
 2560 CLS
 2570 PROC_FRAME
 2580 MOVE X,Y
 2590 ENDPROC
 2600 DEF PROC_PU
 2610 IF WORD$<>"PU" THEN ENDPROC
 2620 PU=1
 2630 ENDPROC
 2640 DEF PROC_PD
 2650 IF WORD$<>"PD" THEN ENDPROC
 2660 PU=0
 2670 ENDPROC
 2680 DEF PROC_SETPOS
 2690 IF WORD$<>"SETPOS" THEN ENDPR
OC
 2700 LOCAL I
 2710 P1$="":P2$=""
 2720 I=0
 2730 I=I+1
 2740 BIT$=MID$(NUM$,I,1)
 2750 IF BIT$=" " THEN 2780
 2760 P1$=P1$+BIT$
 2770 GOTO 2730
 2780 I=I+1
 2790 BIT$=MID$(NUM$,I,1)
 2800 IF I>LEN(NUM$) THEN 2830
 2810 P2$=P2$+BIT$
 2820 GOTO 2780
 2830 PROC_COORD
```

```
 2840 P1=EVAL(P1$):P2=EVAL(P2$)
 2850 P1=P1+COORX:P2=P2+COORY
 2860 IF PU=1 THEN MOVE P1,P2:GOTO
2880
 2870 PLOT PEN,P1,P2
 2880 X=P1:Y=P2
 2890 ENDPROC
 2900 DEF PROC_REPEET
 2910 IF WORD$<>"REPEAT" THEN ENDPR
OC
 2920 IF FLAG0=1 THEN ENDPROC
 2930 LOCAL J:FLAG0=1
 2940 J=0:NI=VAL(NUM$)
 2950 J=J+1
 2960 PROC_COMMAND
 2970 PROC_ANALYSE(A$)
 2980 R$(J)=PRO$
 2990 S$(J)=PAR$
 3000 IF R$(J)="REPEAT" THEN PROC_R
PT
 3010 IF R$(J)="]" THEN 3030
 3020 GOTO 2950
 3030 PROC_EX
 3040 WORD$="VVV"
 3050 FLAG0=0:ENDPROC
 3060 DEF PROC_EX
 3070 LOCAL K,A
 3080 K=0
 3090 FOR A=1 TO NI
 3100   K=K+1
 3110   IF R$(K)="REPEAT" THEN PROC
_EXX
 3120   IF R$(K)="]" THEN K=0:GOTO
3150
 3130   PROC_DO(R$(K),S$(K))
```

123

```
3140    GOTO 3100
3150 NEXT A
3160 ENDPROC
3170 DEF PROC_RPT
3180 LOCAL H
3190 CVAR$=S$(J):PROC_VARCHECK1
3200 ND=EVAL(CVAR$)
3210 H=0
3220 H=H+1
3230 PROC_COMMAND
3240 PROC_ANALYSE(A$)
3250 P$(H)=PRO$
3260 Q$(H)=PAR$
3270 IF P$(H)="]" THEN ENDPROC
3280 GOTO 3220
3290 DEF PROC_EXX
3300 LOCAL F,B
3310 F=0
3320 FOR B=1 TO ND
3330    F=F+1
3340    PROC_DO(P$(F),Q$(F))
3350    IF P$(F)="]" THEN F=0:GOTO
3370
3360    GOTO 3330
3370 NEXT B
3380 ENDPROC
3390 DEF PROC_HT
3400 IF WORD$<>"HT" THEN ENDPROC
3410 PROC_UNTURTLE
3420 HT=1
3430 ENDPROC
3440 DEF PROC_ST
3450 IF WORD$<>"ST" THEN ENDPROC
3460 HT=0
3470 PROC_TURTLE
```

```
3480 ENDPROC
3490 DEF PROC_OP
3500 IF WORD$<>"OP" THEN ENDPROC
3510 IF VARNUM=0 THEN ENDPROC
3520 LOCAL I
3530 I=0
3540 NUM$=":"+MID$(NUM$,2)
3550 I=I+1
3560 IF NAME$(I)<>NUM$ THEN 3590
3570 PRINT TAB(0,2);CL$
3580 PRINT TAB(0,2);EVAL(NAM$(I)):
ENDPROC
3590 IF I<VARNUM THEN 3550
3600 ENDPROC
3610 DEF PROC_MAKE
3620 IF WORD$<>"MAKE" THEN ENDPROC

3630 LOCAL I,PAT,POT,TAZ$,TBZ$
3640 FOR PAT=1 TO VARNUM-1
3650    FOR POT=PAT+1 TO VARNUM
3660       IF LEN(NAME$(PAT))<LEN(NA
ME$(POT)) THEN TAZ$=NAME$(PAT):TBZ$
=NAM$(PAT):NAME$(PAT)=NAME$(POT):NA
M$(PAT)=NAM$(POT):NAME$(POT)=TAZ$:N
AM$(POT)=TBZ$
3670    NEXT POT
3680 NEXT PAT
3690 I=0
3700 NA$=""
3710 NUM$=":"+MID$(NUM$,2)
3720 I=I+1
3730 BIT$=MID$(NUM$,I,1)
3740 IF BIT$=" " THEN 3780
3750 NA$=NA$+BIT$
3760 IF I=LEN(NUM$) THEN ENDPROC
```

125

```
3770 GOTO 3720
3780 I=I+1
3790 VA$=MID$(NUM$,I)
3800 IF VA$="RQ" THEN PRINT TAB(0,
0);CL$:INPUT LINE TAB(0,0);VA$:PRIN
T TAB(0,0);CL$
3810 PROC_PUT
3820 ENDPROC
3830 DEF PROC_PUT
3840 LOCAL I,J,K,FLG
3850 FLG=0
3860 IF VARNUM=0 THEN 3910
3870 FOR I=1 TO VARNUM
3880    IF NAME$(I)=NA$ THEN TEM$=V
A$:FLG=1:K=I
3890 NEXT I
3900 IF FLG=1 THEN 3950
3910 VARNUM=VARNUM+1
3920 NAME$(VARNUM)=NA$
3930 TEM$=VA$
3940 K=VARNUM
3950 LE1=50
3960 FOR J=1 TO VARNUM
3970    NOM$=NAME$(J)
3980    NOME$=NAM$(J)
3990    LL=LEN(NOM$)
4000    FOR I=1 TO LE1
4010       IF MID$(TEM$,I,LL)=NOM$ T
HEN TEM$=MID$(TEM$,1,I-1)+NOME$+MID
$(TEM$,I+LL)
4020    NEXT I
4030 NEXT J
4040 NAM$(K)=TEM$
4050 ENDPROC
4060 DEF PROC_VARCHECK
```

```
 4070 IF VARNUM=Ø THEN ENDPROC
 4080 LOCAL I
 4090 FOR I=1 TO VARNUM
 4100    IF NAME$(I)=NUM$ THEN NUM$=
NAM$(I)
 4110 NEXT I
 4120 ENDPROC
 4130 DEF PROC_COORD
 4140 IF VARNUM=Ø THEN ENDPROC
 4150 LOCAL I
 4160 FOR I=1 TO VARNUM
 4170    IF NAME$(I)=P1$ THEN P1$=NA
M$(I)
 4180    IF NAME$(I)=P2$ THEN P2$=NA
M$(I)
 4190 NEXT I
 4200 ENDPROC
 4210 DEF PROC_TO
 4220 IF WORD$<>"TO" THEN ENDPROC
 4230 E(Ø)=Ø
 4240 CLS:PRINT"TO ";NUM$
 4250 WO=WO+1
 4260 PROC_ANALYSE(NUM$)
 4270 NUM$=PRO$
 4280 W$(WO)=NUM$
 4290 IF PAR$="" THEN 4340
 4300 WA$(WO)=PAR$
 4310 WORD$="MAKE":NUM$=PAR$+" 1"
 4320 NUM$=MID$(NUM$,1)
 4330 PROC_MAKE
 4340 S(WO)=E(WO-1)+1
 4350 INPUT LINE;A$
 4360 PROC_ANALYSE(A$)
 4370 IF PRO$="END" THEN E(WO)=DD:W
ORD$="VVV":NUM$="1":CLS:PROC_FRAME:
MOVE X,Y:ENDPROC
```

127

```
 4380 DD=DD+1
 4390 PR$(DD)=PRO$:PA$(DD)=PAR$
 4400 GOTO 4350
 4410 DEF PROC_LEVEL1(COM$,PAT$)
 4420 IF WO=0 THEN ENDPROC
 4430 FOR I3=1 TO WO
 4440   IF COM$=W$(I3) THEN WORD$="
MAKE":NUM$=WA$(I3)+" "+PAT$:PROC_MA
KE:PROC_EXLEVEL1
 4450 NEXT I3
 4460 ENDPROC
 4470 DEF PROC_EXLEVEL1
 4480 O1=S(I3):O2=E(I3)
 4490 FOR I4=O1 TO O2
 4500    PROC_DO1(PR$(I4),PA$(I4))
 4510 NEXT I4
 4520 ENDPROC
 4530 DEF PROC_SETPC
 4540 IF WORD$<>"SETPC" THEN ENDPRO
C
 4550 COL=EVAL(NUM$)
 4560 GCOL 129,COL
 4570 ENDPROC
 4580 DEF PROC_REPEET1
 4590 IF WORD$<>"REPEAT" THEN ENDPR
OC
 4600 IF FLAG1=1 THEN ENDPROC
 4610 LOCAL JJ
 4620 JJ=0:FLAG1=1
 4630 IF PA$(I4)="" THEN PA$(I4)="0
"
 4640 CVAR$=PA$(I4):PROC_VARCHECK1
 4650 NI1=EVAL(CVAR$)
 4660 JJ=JJ+1
 4670 I4=I4+1
```

```
4680 RR$(JJ)=PR$(I4)
4690 SS$(JJ)=PA$(I4)
4700 IF RR$(JJ)="REPEAT" THEN PROC
_RPT1
4710 IF RR$(JJ)="]" THEN 4730
4720 GOTO 4660
4730 PROC_EX1
4740 FLAG1=0:ENDPROC
4750 DEF PROC_RPT1
4760 LOCAL L4
4770 CVAR$=SS$(JJ):PROC_VARCHECK1
4780 NE=EVAL(CVAR$)
4790 L4=0
4800 L4=L4+1
4810 I4=I4+1
4820 PP$(L4)=PR$(I4)
4830 QQ$(L4)=PA$(I4)
4840 IF PP$(L4)="]" THEN ENDPROC
4850 GOTO 4800
4860 DEF PROC_EX1
4870 LOCAL KK,AA
4880 KK=0
4890 FOR AA=1 TO NI1
4900    KK=KK+1
4910    IF RR$(KK)="REPEAT" THEN PR
OC_EXX1
4920    IF RR$(KK)="]" THEN KK=0:GO
TO 4950
4930    PROC_DO1(RR$(KK),SS$(KK))
4940    GOTO 4900
4950 NEXT AA
4960 ENDPROC
4970 DEF PROC_EXX1
4980 LOCAL FF,BB
4990 FF=0
```

129

```
5000 FOR BB=1 TO NE
5010    FF=FF+1
5020    PROC_DO1(PP$(FF),QQ$(FF))
5030    IF PP$(FF)="]" THEN FF=0:GO
TO 5050
5040    GOTO 5010
5050 NEXT BB
5060 ENDPROC
5070 DEF PROC_DO1(XX$,YY$)
5080 NUM$=YY$
5090 WORD$=XX$
5100 LEVEL=1:GOTO 8170
5110 IF XX$="STOPIF" THEN 5470
5120 PROC_ORIGIN
5130 IF XX$="ORIGIN" THEN 5470
5140 PROC_CT
5150 PROC_PR
5160 PROC_MAKE
5170 IF WORD$="MAKE" THEN ENDPROC
5180 PROC_OP
5190 IF WORD$="OP" THEN ENDPROC
5200 PROC_UNTURTLE
5210 PROC_SETPOS
5220 IF WORD$="SETPOS" THEN 5470
5230 IF NUM$="" THEN NUM$="1"
5240 PROC_VARCHECK
5250 PAR=EVAL(NUM$)
5260 PROC_SETY
5270 PROC_SETX
5280 PROC_SETPC
5290 PROC_REPEET1
5300 PROC_FD(PEN)
5310 PROC_BK
5320 PROC_RT
5330 PROC_LT
```

```
 5340 PROC_CS
 5350 PROC_PU
 5360 PROC_PD
 5370 PROC_HT
 5380 PROC_ST
 5390 PROC_PE
 5400 PROC_DASHED
 5410 PROC_DOTTED
 5420 PROC_SOLID
 5430 PROC_CIRCLE
 5440 PROC_FILL
 5450 PROC_HOME
 5460 PROC_CLEAN
 5470 PROC_TURTLE
 5480 PROC_LEVEL2(WORD$,NUM$)
 5490 WORD$="VVV":NUM$="VVV":PAR=Ø
 5500 ENDPROC
 5510 DEF PROC_LEVEL2(COMM$,PATT$)
 5520 FOR I5=1 TO WO
 5530    IF COMM$=W$(I5) THEN WORD$=
"MAKE":NUM$=WA$(I5)+" "+PATT$:PROC_
MAKE:PROC_EXLEVEL2
 5540 NEXT I5
 5550 ENDPROC
 5560 DEF PROC_EXLEVEL2
 5570 O3=S(I5):O4=E(I5)
 5580 FOR I6=O3 TO O4
 5590    PROC_DO2(PR$(I6),PA$(I6))
 5600 NEXT I6
 5610 ENDPROC
 5620 DEF PROC_REPEET2
 5630 IF WORD$<>"REPEAT" THEN ENDPR
OC
 5640 IF FLAG2=1 THEN ENDPROC
 5650 LOCAL LL
```

131

```
  5660 LL=Ø:FLAG2=1
  5670 IF PA$(I6)="" THEN PA$(I6)="Ø
"
  5680 CVAR$=PA$(I6):PROC_VARCHECK1
  5690 NI2=EVAL(CVAR$)
  5700 LL=LL+1
  5710 I6=I6+1
  5720 RRR$(LL)=PR$(I6)
  5730 SSS$(LL)=PA$(I6)
  5740 IF RRR$(LL)="REPEAT" THEN PRO
C_RPT2
  5750 IF RRR$(LL)="]" THEN 5770
  5760 GOTO 5700
  5770 PROC_EX2
  5780 FLAG2=Ø:ENDPROC
  5790 DEF PROC_RPT2
  5800 LOCAL L6
  5810 CVAR$=SSS$(LL):PROC_VARCHECK1

  5820 NF=EVAL(CVAR$)
  5830 L6=Ø
  5840 L6=L6+1
  5850 I6=I6+1
  5860 PPP$(L6)=PR$(I6)
  5870 QQQ$(L6)=PA$(I6)
  5880 IF PPP$(L6)="]" THEN ENDPROC
  5890 GOTO 5840
  5900 DEF PROC_EX2
  5910 LOCAL MM,CC
  5920 MM=Ø
  5930 FOR CC=1 TO NI2
  5940     MM=MM+1
  5950     IF RRR$(MM)="REPEAT" THEN P
ROC_EXX2
```

```
5960    IF RRR$(MM)="]" THEN MM=0:G
OTO 5990
5970    PROC_DO2(RRR$(MM),SSS$(MM))

5980    GOTO 5940
5990 NEXT CC
6000 ENDPROC
6010 DEF PRC_EXX2
6020 LOCAL NN,DD
6030 NN=0
6040 FOR DD=1 TO NF
6050    NN=NN+1
6060    PROC_DO2(PPP$(NN),QQQ$(NN))

6070    IF PPP$(NN)="]" THEN NN=0:G
OTO 6090
6080    GOTO 6050
6090 NEXT DD
6100 ENDPROC
6110 DEF PROC_DO2(XXX$,YYY$)
6120 NUM$=YYY$
6130 WORD$=XXX$
6140 LEVEL=2:GOTO 8170
6150 IF XXX$="STOPIF" THEN 6510
6160 PROC_ORIGIN
6170 IF XXX$="ORIGIN" THEN 6510
6180 PROC_CT
6190 PROC_PR
6200 PROC_MAKE
6210 IF WORD$="MAKE" THEN ENDPROC
6220 PROC_OP
6230 IF WORD$="OP" THEN ENDPROC
6240 PROC_UNTURTLE
6250 PROC_SETPOS
6260 IF WORD$="SETPOS" THEN 6510
```

```
6270 IF NUM$="" THEN NUM$="1"
6280 PROC_VARCHECK
6290 PAR=EVAL(NUM$)
6300 PROC_SETY
6310 PROC_SETX
6320 PROC_SETPC
6330 PROC_REPEET2
6340 PROC_FD(PEN)
6350 PROC_BK
6360 PROC_RT
6370 PROC_LT
6380 PROC_CS
6390 PROC_PU
6400 PROC_PD
6410 PROC_HT
6420 PROC_ST
6430 PROC_PE
6440 PROC_DASHED
6450 PROC_DOTTED
6460 PROC_SOLID
6470 PROC_CIRCLE
6480 PROC_FILL
6490 PROC_HOME
6500 PROC_CLEAN
6510 PROC_TURTLE
6520 WORD$="VVV":NUM$="VVV":PAR=0
6530 ENDPROC
6540 DEF PROC_VARCHECK1
6550 IF VARNUM=0 THEN ENDPROC
6560 LOCAL I
6570 FOR I=1 TO VARNUM
6580    IF NAME$(I)=CVAR$ THEN CVAR
$=NAM$(I)
6590 NEXT I
6600 ENDPROC
```

```
6610 DEF PROC_CLEAN
6620 IF WORD$<>"CLEAN" THEN ENDPRO
C
6630 CLS
6640 PROC_FRAME
6650 MOVE X,Y
6660 ENDPROC
6670 DEF PROC_HOME
6680 IF WORD$<>"HOME" THEN ENDPROC

6690 PROC_UNTURTLE
6700 X=512:Y=335:CURRENT=90:ANGLE=
90:TEMP=0:XX=0:YY=0
6710 MOVE X,Y
6720 ENDPROC
6730 DEF PROC_PE
6740 IF WORD$<>"PE" THEN ENDPROC
6750 GCOL 132,0
6760 ENDPROC
6770 DEF PROC_FILL
6780 IF WORD$<>"FILL" THEN ENDPROC

6790 PLOT 101,X,Y
6800 ENDPROC
6810 DEF PROC_POTS
6820 IF WORD$<>"POTS" THEN ENDPROC

6830 CLS
6840 LOCAL I
6850 FOR I=1 TO WO
6860    PRINT W$(I);WA$(I)
6870 NEXT I
6880 COLOUR 11
6890 PRINT"ENTER 'P' TO CONTINUE"
6900 COLOUR 15
```

```
  6910 INPUT KE$:IF KE$<>"P" THEN 68
90
  6920 CLS
  6930 PROC_FRAME
  6940 MOVE X,Y
  6950 PROC_TURTLE
  6960 ENDPROC
  6970 DEF PROC_PONS
  6980 IF WORD$<>"PONS" THEN ENDPROC

  6990 CLS
  7000 IF VARNUM<1 THEN 7050
  7010 LOCAL I
  7020 FOR I=1 TO VARNUM
  7030    PRINT MID$(NAME$(I),2);" ";
EVAL(NAM$(I))
  7040 NEXT I
  7050 COLOUR 11
  7060 PRINT"ENTER 'P' TO CONTINUE"
  7070 COLOUR 15
  7080 INPUT KE$:IF KE$<>"P" THEN 70
60
  7090 CLS
  7100 PROC_FRAME
  7110 MOVE X,Y
  7120 PROC_TURTLE
  7130 ENDPROC
  7140 DEF PROC_PO
  7150 IF WORD$<>"PO" THEN ENDPROC
  7160 LOCAL I
  7170 PROC_ANALYSE(NUM$)
  7180 I=0
  7190 PRO$=MID$(PRO$,2)
  7200 I=I+1
```

```
 7210 IF W$(I)=PRO$ AND WA$(I)=PAR$
  THEN 7240
 7220 IF I=WO THEN PRINT TAB(0,1);C
L$:PRINT TAB(0,1);"NOT FOUND":ENDPR
OC
 7230 GOTO 7200
 7240 CLS
 7250 PRINT"TO ";PRO$;" ";PAR$
 7260 FOR J=S(I) TO E(I)
 7270    PRINT PR$(J);" ";PA$(J)
 7280 NEXT J
 7290 COLOUR 11
 7300 PRINT"ENTER 'P' TO PROCEED"
 7310 COLOUR 15
 7320 INPUT KE$:IF KE$<>"P" THEN 72
90
 7330 CLS
 7340 PROC_FRAME
 7350 MOVE X,Y
 7360 PROC_TURTLE
 7370 ENDPROC
 7380 DEF PROC_PR
 7390 IF WORD$<>"PR" THEN ENDPROC
 7400 PRINT TAB(0,2);CL$
 7410 PRINT TAB(0,2);MID$(NUM$,2,LE
N(NUM$)-2)
 7420 NUM$="0"
 7430 ENDPROC
 7440 DEF PROC_CT
 7450 IF WORD$<>"CT" THEN ENDPROC
 7460 PRINT TAB(0,0);CL$
 7470 PRINT TAB(0,1);CL$
 7480 PRINT TAB(0,2);CL$
 7490 NUM$="0":ENDPROC
 7500 DEF PROC_SETY
 7510 IF WORD$<>"SETY" THEN ENDPROC
```

```
7520 Y=EVAL(NUM$)+COORY
7530 PLOT PEN,X,Y
7540 ENDPROC
7550 DEF PROC_SETX
7560 IF WORD$<>"SETX" THEN ENDPROC

7570 X=EVAL(NUM$)+COORX
7580 PLOT PEN,X,Y
7590 ENDPROC
7600 DEF PROC_ED
7610 IF WORD$<>"ED" THEN ENDPROC
7620 LOCAL I
7630 PROC_ANALYSE(NUM$)
7640 I=Ø
7650 PRO$=MID$(PRO$,2)
7660 I=I+1
7670 IF W$(I)=PRO$ AND WA$(I)=PAR$
THEN 7700
7680 IF I=WO THEN PRINT TAB(Ø,1);C
L$:PRINT TAB(Ø,1);"NOT FOUND":ENDFR
OC
7690 GOTO 7660
7700 CLS
7710 PRINT"TO ";PRO$;" ";PAR$
7720 FOR J=S(I) TO E(I)
7730    PRINT"#";J-(S(I)-1);" ";PR$
(J);" ";PA$(J)
7740 NEXT J
7750 COLOUR 11
7760 PRINT"ENTER 'P' TO PROCEED"
7770 PRINT" OR 'E' TO EDIT"
7780 COLOUR 15
7790 INPUT KE$
7800 IF KE$="P" THEN 7830
7810 IF KE$="E" THEN 7880
```

```
7820 GOTO 7750
7830 CLS
7840 PROC_FRAME
7850 MOVE X,Y
7860 PROC_TURTLE
7870 ENDPROC
7880 COLOUR 11:PRINT"ENTER #NUMBER
OF LINE TO BE EDITED":COLOUR 7
7890 INPUT HN
7900 HN=HN+S(I)
7910 COLOUR 11:PRINT"ENTER REPLACE
MENT LINE":COLOUR 7
7920 INPUT LINE LI$
7930 COLOUR 15
7940 PROC_ANALYSE(LI$)
7950 PR$(S(J)+HN-1)=PRO$:PA$(S(J)+
HN-1)=PAR$
7960 GOTO 7720
7970 REM ALL HIGHER LINE NUMBERS A
RE EXTRA
7980 DEF PROC_CIRCLE
7990 IF WORD$<>"CIRCLE" THEN ENDPR
OC
8000 PLOT 37,PAR,PAR
8010 ENDPROC
8020 DEF PROC_DASHED
8030 IF WORD$<>"DASHED" THEN ENDPR
OC
8040 PEN=21
8050 ENDPROC
8060 DEF PROC_DOTTED
8070 IF WORD$<>"DOTTED" THEN ENDPR
OC
8080 PEN=13
8090 ENDPROC
```

139

```
 8100 DEF PROC_SOLID
 8110 IF WORD$<>"SOLID" THEN ENDPRO
C
 8120 PEN=5
 8130 ENDPROC
 8140 REM DESTINATION FOR ERRORS
 8150 RUN
 8160 PRINT TAB(0,2);"PROCEDURE TER
MINATED":FOR I=1 TO 2000:NEXT I:PRI
NT TAB(0,2);CL$:A=50:B=50:AA=50:BB=
50:CC=50:DD=50:ENDPROC
 8170 REM STOPIF
 8180 IF WORD$<>"STOPIF" THEN 8220
 8190 TTT$=":TA":TEST$=NUM$:WORD$="
MAKE":NUM$=TTT$+" "+TEST$
 8200 PROC_MAKE
 8210 IF EVAL(TEM$)=-1 THEN 8160
 8220 IF LEVEL=0 THEN 1630
 8230 IF LEVEL=1 THEN 5110
 8240 IF LEVEL=2 THEN 6150
 8250 DEF PROC_ORIGIN
 8260 IF WORD$<>"ORIGIN" THEN ENDPR
OC
 8270 IF NUM$="MID" THEN COORX=512:
COORY=335
 8280 IF NUM$="BL" THEN COORX=0:COO
RY=0
 8290 ENDPROC
 8300 DEF PROC_FILE
 8310 IF WORD$<>"FILE" THEN ENDPROC

 8320 FILE=OPENOUT(NUM$+".TRT")
 8330 PRINT#FILE,STR$(WO)
 8340 FOR I=1 TO WO
 8350    PRINT#FILE,W$(I)
```

```
8360    PRINT#FILE,WA$(I)
8370    PRINT#FILE,STR$(S(I))
8380    PRINT#FILE,STR$(E(I))
8390 NEXT I
8400 PRINT#FILE,STR$(DD)
8410 FOR I=1 TO DD
8420    PRINT#FILE,PR$(I)
8430    PRINT#FILE,PA$(I)
8440 NEXT I
8450 CLOSE#FILE
8460 PRINT TAB(Ø,2);CL$
8470 PRINT TAB(Ø,2);NUM$;".TRT FIL
ED"
8480 ENDPROC
8490 DEF PROC_LOADD
8500 IF WORD$<>"LOAD" THEN ENDPROC

8510 FILE=OPENIN(NUM$)
8520 INPUT#FILE,WWW$
8530 WO=EVAL(WWW$)
8540 FOR I=1 TO WO
8550    INPUT#FILE,W$(I)
8560    INPUT#FILE,WA$(I)
8570    INPUT#FILE,WWW$
8580    S(I)=EVAL(WWW$)
8590    INPUT#FILE,WWW$
8600    E(I)=EVAL(WWW$)
8610 NEXT I
8620 INPUT#FILE,WWW$
8630 DD=EVAL(WWW$)
8640 FOR I=1 TO DD
8650    INPUT#FILE,PR$(I)
8660    INPUT#FILE,PA$(I)
8670 NEXT I
8680 CLOSE#FILE
```

```
 8690 PRINT TAB(0,2);CL$
 8700 PRINT TAB(0,2);NUM$;" LOADED"

 8710 ENDPROC
>*OPT 0
```

ALSO AVAILABLE

BASIC & PASCAL IN PARALLEL   **BP126**
S.J. Wainwright, B.Sc., Ph.D., M.I.Biol, C.Biol.

This book takes the two languages BASIC and Pascal, and develops programs in both languages simultaneously. Emphasis is placed on structured programming by the systematic use of control structures; and modular program design is used throughout. Example programs are used to illustrate the program structures as they are introduced, and the reader can learn by example.

If the book is used as an introduction to BASIC programming, the structured approach will encourage good programming techniques which will be compatible with Pascal programming at a later date, and will eliminate many of the difficulties commonly met by BASIC programmers when they move over to programming in Pascal, and have to rethink their approach to program design. BASIC is used to emulate Pascal throughout the text, so the transition from BASIC to Pascal should present few problems to a person who can already program in BASIC.

If the book is used as an introduction to Pascal programming, the presence of equivalent programs in BASIC but having Pascal-like structure, will provide a familiar BASIC "handle" with which to grasp the Pascal programming techniques. If the reader does not yet possess a Pascal interpreter or compiler, he/she can learn many of the features of Pascal by using the BASIC programs on his/her own computer, and comparing them with the Pascal listings.

The common ground between the BASIC and Pascal programming languages is covered, and emphasis is placed on the similarities rather than the differences between them. As the title suggests, the book is intended as a bilingual introduction to programming which can be used to learn programming in both languages simultaneously, and to learn programming techniques which are compatible with both languages.

0 85934 101 1   64 pages   178 x 111 mm   1983   £1.50

BASIC & FORTRAN IN PARALLEL   BP137
S.J. Wainwright, B.Sc., Ph.D., M.I.Biol, C.Biol.
& A.Grant, B.Sc.

This book could be used to learn FORTRAN; it could be
used to learn BASIC. It could also be used to learn both
languages at the same time.

FORTRAN is an acronym for FORmula TRANslation.
It was developed in the mid 1950s and was one of the first
high-level languages to be developed, and the first to be used
extensively. This historical accident has meant that
FORTRAN occupies a position of importance; with much
programming, particularly for scientific purposes, being done
in FORTRAN. It is unlikely to be dislodged from this
position in the near future, if ever, as so much time and money
has been invested in writing FORTRAN programs. At the
time of writing, FORTRAN is available on at least 70 microcomputers, and this number is likely to increase.

As an appendix to this book, we have included a FOR-
TRAN interpreter written in Sinclair Spectrum BASIC, which
should also run with little modification on the Sinclair ZX81.
This supports most of the commonly used features of
FORTRAN, and makes it possible to "get a feel" of what
writing programs in FORTRAN is like.

0 85934 112 7   96 pages   178 x 111 mm   1984   £1.95

BASIC & FORTH IN PARALLEL   BP138
S.J. Wainwright, B.Sc., Ph.D., M.I.Biol., C.Biol.

FORTH is a very different type of language from BASIC,
and has a different philosophy of program development.
However, despite the differences, this book takes both languages together and investigates how things are done in each of
them; BASIC being used as a familiar "handle" with which to
grasp the various programming techniques available in both
languages.

The FORTH-stack simulator which is presented at the end
of the book, will run on either a 16K or 48K Sinclair
Spectrum, and will enable the user to visualise what happens

on the Stack, when the various Stack operator words are used. The Stack is central to the operation of FORTH, and an understanding of the Stack and the Stack effects of FORTH words, is fundamental to an understanding of the FORTH programming language.

0 85934 113 5   112 pages   178 x 111 mm   1984   **£1.95**

Notes

Please note following is a list of other titles that are available in our range of Radio, Electronics and Computer Books.

These should be available from all good Booksellers, Radio Component Dealers and Mail Order Companies.

However, should you experience difficulty in obtaining any title in your area, then please write directly to the Publisher enclosing payment to cover the cost of the book plus adequate postage.

If you would like a complete catalogue of our entire range of Radio, Electronics and Computer Books then please send a Stamped Addressed Envelope to:

BERNARD BABANI (publishing) LTD
THE GRAMPIANS
SHEPHERDS BUSH ROAD
LONDON W6 7NF
ENGLAND